Soviet views on John Maynard Keynes

To Alison Mary

An analysis of Soviet views on John Maynard Keynes

Carl B. Turner

Duke University Press   *Durham, North Carolina*   *1969*

Printed in the United States of America by Heritage Printers, Inc.

Preface

The purpose of this study is to analyze the Soviet criticism of John Maynard Keynes and his major works from the founding of the Soviet state in 1917 to the retirement of Khrushchev in October, 1964. In view of the length of the period covered, research was concentrated on Soviet materials that emphasized bourgeois political economy. Despite this restriction, the materials concerning Keynes were extensive enough to preclude the treatment of all the works in detail. As a result only the most important books and articles on Keynes have been given prominence and the remainder introduced briefly to develop the pattern of Soviet criticism of Keynes during the period under investigation. A considerable quantity of further literature was reviewed but not cited directly in this study since it contributed little of further significance to the topic. Much of the Soviet criticism of bourgeois political economy is, as can be imagined, highly polemic and extremely repetitive, so a representative selection is sufficient to show the general trend.

The plan of the study is broadly chronological: Chapter I deals with the background to Soviet criticism on Keynes; Chapter II treats the early views on Keynes with emphasis on Lenin's references to him; Chapter III reviews the Soviet position on Keynes from 1936 to the appearance of the Russian translation of *The General Theory* in 1948; Chapter IV analyzes the expurgated Russian edition of *The General Theory*; Chapter V surveys the Soviet criticism of Keynes during the height of the cold war; Chapter VI shows the extent of his influence as seen by the Soviets; Chapter VII evaluates the Soviet estimate of him during the Khrushchev period; and Chapter VIII contains the general conclusion of the study.

There were difficulties in obtaining Soviet materials, as files of Soviet journals for the early period were found to be incomplete even in the largest libraries in the West. However, research during a period covering two and a half years, which included a visit to the Soviet Union during the summer of 1963, produced a collection of materials sufficient to undertake this study. The emphasis has been predominantly on primary sources that were not available in translation. The translations of the

Soviet sources are therefore my own, and I take full responsibility for them. They keep as closely as possible to the original, though I have tried to relieve them of any awkwardness. Where known, the official status of the Soviet economists has been given, but it is exceedingly difficult to identify most Soviet authors since generally only the name and initials are given without any indication of affiliation to any institution.

I wish to acknowledge my considerable debt to Professor Calvin B. Hoover of Duke University. Without his constant counsel and generous support this study would not have been possible. He sponsored the trip to the Soviet Union during the summer of 1963 that enabled me to obtain certain materials for this study not available in the West. I am also indebted to Professors Joseph J. Spengler, Robert S. Smith, Frank T. de Vyver, and John S. Curtiss, likewise of Duke University, for helpful suggestions in the discussion of the problems encountered in this study. Lastly, I gratefully acknowledge the generous support of the Committee on Publications of the Graduate School of Arts and Sciences of Duke University.

C. B. T.

Contents

Soviet views on John Maynard Keynes

I. *Introduction: The background to Soviet criticism of Keynes*

Probably no economist since Adam Smith and David Ricardo has had such a devoted following in the Western World as John Maynard Keynes. His writings had drawn considerable comment even before the publication of *The General Theory of Employment, Interest and Money* in 1936.[1] With the appearance of this work, however, Keynes's ideas aroused a volume both of support and of controversy among economists and statesmen throughout the world which far surpassed that accorded to his earlier writings.

It is not surprising, therefore, to find that Keynes has attracted considerable Soviet attention as well. It would be very strange indeed if the Soviets did not recognize him, considering his influence in the West. Yet Soviet economists rarely attempt any lengthy analysis of a single Western economist. They base their analysis on Marxian doctrine, which supposedly contains the analytical tools that enable them to discover scientifically the objective laws of economic development. Lacking this scientific means of analysis, the overwhelming majority of the Western economists, in the Soviet view, are "vulgar"[2] economists who can deal only subjectively with economic phenomena, and so their analysis and apologetics can be conveniently dismissed out of hand as superficial.

A review of Soviet economic and political journals will yield a large number of articles on capitalism. Soviet economists tend to

---

1. John M. Keynes, *The General Theory of Employment, Interest and Money* (London, 1936). Hereinafter cited as *The General Theory*.
2. The Soviets are fond of the term *vulgar*. It derives from Marx, who wrote: "The vulgar economist does practically no more than translate the singular concepts of the capitalists, who are in the thrall of competition, into a seemingly more theoretical and generalized language, and attempt to substantiate the justice of those concepts." Karl Marx, *Capital*, III (Moscow, 1962), 226. The term as used by the Soviets is clearly derogatory, but in the sense of unenlightened or superficial, rather than common or crude.

treat capitalism as a system and discuss general topics such as crises, unemployment, and the growth of monopoly. At times they will review particular theories or contributions of prominent Western economists, but this has not frequently been the case. When Western economists have been discussed, generally they have been conveniently banded together regardless of interests or speciality; for example, both Alvin Hansen and Milton Friedman are considered as upholders of unemployment.[3] Keynes is one of the rare exceptions to this rule. There have been an unprecedented number of references, articles, and even books on Keynes and his theory. His main works have been translated into Russian and have gone through several printings. In this respect, he stands apart from his Western colleagues.

Even the terminology used about Keynes is as extensive in the East as it is in the West. Keynes and all the variations derived from his name have been transliterated into Russian. Since the Russian language is highly inflected, the outcome even exceeds the variety found in English. The literature reviewed contains the terms Keins (Keynes), Keinsianets (Keynesian—i.e., a follower of Keynes), Keinsianstvo (Keynesianism), Keinsianskii (Keynesian—adjective), as well as the following both in the noun and adjectival forms: neo-Keynesian, left Keynesian, contemporary Keynesian, radical Keynesian, and orthodox Keynesian.

The references to Keynes or to his works have been in evidence throughout the Soviet period. Lenin himself referred to Keynes in three of his reports.[4] In fact, in his "Report on the International Situation and the Basic Tasks of the Communist International," he conveniently borrowed from Keynes's *The Economic Consequences of the Peace* for his own arguments in regard to the impending collapse of the capitalist West.[5] This report was delivered to the Second Congress of the Communist International on July 19, 1920, in Petrograd. This would have been enough to distinguish Keynes in the eyes of Soviet economists, and Lenin's numerous references to Keynes

3. I. G. Blyumin, *Ocherki sovremennoi burzhuaznoi politicheskoi ekonomii SShA* (Moskva, 1956), chap. ii.
4. Lenin's remarks on Keynes will be discussed in chap. ii.
5. V. I. Lenin, *Sochineniya*, 4th ed.; XXXI (Moskva, 1950), 191–209.

have been regularly used by Soviet economists and journalists to the present.

However, with the appearance of *The General Theory*, Keynes's position took on new meaning in the East as well as in the West. The chief significance of *The General Theory* was its contention that full employment was obtainable if the forces of the economic system were fully understood and if the state were to undertake certain functions regarding effective demand and investment. This, in turn, would continue to make capitalism a viable system—a contention, of course, that is anathema to the Soviets. Since this work served as the theoretical basis for a new approach to economics in the West, the Soviets could not readily ignore it or the man behind it. Slowly at first, but with increasing regularity, articles on Keynes and his theory appeared.

The General Theory was translated into Russian in 1948 with a second printing in 1949. These editions are constantly referred to by Soviet writers in their works on Keynes and in their treatment of Western economic theories in general. In 1953 a book by V. S. Volodin was devoted entirely to Keynes.[6] Volodin concentrated his effort mainly on *The General Theory*, and it is the most extensive critique of Keynes in the Soviet Union. This was published at the height of the cold war and shows clearly the Soviet position with respect to him at this time.

After the death of Stalin and the rise of Khrushchev, the Soviets devoted increasing attention and criticism to bourgeois economic theory, and in particular to the spread of Keynesian influence. This was a result of the historic Twentieth Party Congress of February, 1956, when Khrushchev gave his formal approval to the policy of peaceful coexistence. However, it should be emphasized that Khrushchev's words applied primarily to the avoidance of open military conflict and not to the ideological struggle between East and West, or, to put the matter in Soviet terms, between socialism and capitalism, which was to be waged as intensively as theretofore. Increasing emphasis was thus placed on competition in the sphere of economic

---

6. V. S. Volodin, *Keins—ideolog monopolisticheskogo kapitala* (Moskva, 1953). This work will be analyzed in chap. v.

systems, and the Soviets were forced to examine more closely the economic theories of their adversaries.

At the Conference of the Representatives of the Eighty-One Communist and Workers' Parties held in Moscow in November, 1960, after a general statement about the "struggle between the two opposing social systems,"[7] the delegates went on to discuss the general trends in world capitalism. Their analysis led to the official recognition of what they regarded as a third stage in the "general crisis of capitalism." Among the numerous factors considered to have produced this new stage were the triumph of socialism in a large number of countries, the weakening of imperialism, the growth of the national liberation movements, the instability of the capitalist system, the sharpening contradictions of capitalism, the development of state-monopoly capitalism, the growth of militarism, the failure of bourgeois democracy, and the deepening crisis in bourgeois ideology. All the above was taken as evidence of the fact that *a new stage has begun in the development of the general crisis of capitalism.*"[8]

This third stage was analyzed at length by Academician A. A. Arzumanyan in a monograph entitled *The New Stage in the General Crisis of Capitalism.*[9] The distinguishing features of this stage were twofold: first, that there was no necessity of world wars to disseminate the ideas of socialism,[10] and second, that this stage itself had arisen not from world wars, as had the previous stages, but as a result of the competition between the two systems.[11] Hence, the new stage fitted neatly into the general policy of peaceful coexistence.

Forced to account for the survival of capitalism despite the upheavals of two world wars, the Soviets have had to ask themselves who or what has been responsible for prolonging its existence. Hence their current interest in Keynes and Keynesianism, which they have identified as the primary source of the modifications of capitalism that have taken place since the thirties and that have insured its sur-

---

7. *Pravda*, Dec. 6, 1960, p. 1.   8. *Ibid.*
9. A. A. Arzumanyan, *Novyi etap obshchego krizisa kapitalizma* (Moskva, 1961).
10. *Ibid.*, p. 29.   11. *Pravda*, Dec. 6, 1960, p. 1.

vival. The Soviet writers who specialize in the criticism of bourgeois political economy have studied and rejected all the many varied forms of capitalism in the West. A study of their economic literature revealed their awareness of the following types: new, transformed, crisis-free, democratic, dynamic, people's, planned, organized, contemporary, regulated, permanent, flourishing, mixed, old-style, and new-style. The Soviets, however, have simplified the matter and are in agreement that the above are only forms of one capitalism. Capitalism itself, according to the Soviets, has not changed regardless of what it is called in the West. From their viewpoint, it is distinguished by the institution of private property, the incentive of profit making, and production for the market. In dealing with capitalism, the Soviets have not broken ranks and split into denominations as economists have in the West.

Keynes, whose theory is seen to be at the basis of the main school of contemporary capitalism, has been recognized by the Soviets as the chief ideologist of the West in the area of political economy. This is best illustrated by the following quotation from an article by Dvorkin, one of the chief contemporary Soviet critics of bourgeois political economy:

After World War II the spread of Keynesian theories among bourgeois circles was without parallel. Keynes was glorified both by economists and by bourgeois politicians, now as a prophet, now as the "greatest genius" of economic science, now as the savior of capitalism. Keynes's prescriptions became in effect the practical program of capitalist states in the West.[12]

The purpose of the present study is to analyze in detail the evolution of Soviet criticism of John Maynard Keynes from Lenin through the rule of Khrushchev. In view of the high esteem in which Keynes and his theory are held today in the West, such a study seems particularly relevant. Besides this general interest, there are two further considerations in assessing the value of such an analysis. First, it is hoped that it will contribute to the general understanding of the development of Soviet criticism of bourgeois political economy and

12. I. N. Dvorkin, *Tekhnicheskii progress i burzhuaznaya politekonomiya* (Moskva, 1961), p. 5.

help to identify some of the leading Soviet critics in this field and their respective positions with regard to the West. Second, since the economic struggle between the two systems involves the theoretical as well as the practical side of economics, it is felt that a study of our adversaries' case against our system may help to indicate the best means of meeting their criticisms.

II. *Early Soviet views of Keynes prior to* The General Theory

This period covers the early years of the Soviet Union, marked by upheavals and wars—a period that saw the New Economic Policy, the struggles for leadership, the economic debates, the five-year plans, and forced collectivization. It also witnessed the death of Lenin, the defeat of Trotsky, and the victory of Stalin.

Lenin, himself a prodigious writer, was aware of Keynes and was well acquainted with his *Economic Consequences of the Peace*.[1] In fact, on June 29, 1920, Lenin had instructed the Central Committee of the RKP to have it published in Russian: "Order the State publishing house to publish quickly (with abridgments) Keynes's book *The Economic Consequences of the Peace*."[2] Lenin made extensive references to this book in a speech entitled "A Report on the International Situation and the Basic Tasks of the Communist International,"[3] delivered to the Second Congress of the Communist International on July 19, 1920, in Petrograd. In it he dealt at length with the world international situation.

Lenin noticed the contradictions that were sharpening within the victorious nations and proceeded to give some illustrations of this development:

Take the national debts. We know that the debts of the main European states have grown from 1914 to 1920 not less than *seven* times. I shall introduce still another economic source that acquires especially great significance. This is Keynes, the English diplomat and author of the book *The Economic Consequences of the Peace*. On the instructions of his government, he participated in the negotiations of the Versailles Treaty, observed the negotiations directly with a pure bourgeois point of view, studied the matter step by step in detail, and participated in the meetings as

1. New York, 1920.
2. *Leninskii sbornik*, 3rd ed.; XXXV (Moskva, 1945), 134. The translation of Keynes's book was finally published in 1922, but in an unabridged version.
3. V. I. Lenin, *Sochineniya*, XXXI, 191–209.

an economist. He came to conclusions that are more powerful, more striking, and more edifying than any conclusion a communist-revolutionary could draw. This is because the conclusions were given by an avowed bourgeois, a ruthless opponent of bolshevism, which he, as an English philistine, pictures in an ugly, savage, and brutal manner. Keynes came to the conclusion that Europe and the entire world are destined for bankruptcy. Keynes resigned, and he threw his book in the face of the government and said: "You are acting like madmen."[4]

Lenin discussed the international financial position of the victorious countries. British assets included loans to Imperial Russia. Lenin noted that Keynes did not think these loans would be repaid. According to Lenin, the Russian representative, Krassin, told Lloyd George that the British were harboring delusions if they expected payment.[5] Lenin settled the matter: "as you know these debts do not disturb us because we followed the excellent advice of Keynes a little earlier than the appearance of his book and canceled all debts. [Stormy applause.]"[6]

Keynes had proposed that all Inter-Ally debts be canceled.[7] France would gain, Britain would not lose very much, but America would lose a fair amount. Lenin thought Keynes mistaken in depending on American generosity in writing off her loans to Europe, but he agreed that the United States would have difficulty carrying on international trade as long as the burden of reparations and war debts remained. "And this Keynes who has passed through all the trials of the Versailles negotiations is forced to admit this impossibility despite all his unyielding determination to defend capitalism and despite all his hatred toward bolshevism."[8]

Lenin praised Keynes for his accuracy in depicting Woodrow Wilson. "By the way I do not think that even a communist or general revolutionary proclamation could on its own merits compare with the pages in Keynes where he pictures Wilson and Wilsonism in practice."[9] Lenin thought that even "pedants" could see from Keynes's book that Wilson did not understand the class struggle.

4. *Ibid.*, XXXI, 194–195.
5. *Ibid.*, XXXI, 195.   6. *Ibid.*, XXXI, 196.
7. *Economic Consequences of the Peace*, p. 270.
8. Lenin, *Sochineniya*, XXXI, 198–199.
9. *Ibid.*, XXXI, 199.

Lenin continued the theme of the class struggle. He maintained that thousands of people would follow the example of Keynes, who had resigned and thrown his book in the government's face. He again introduced the topic of the cancellation of all debts that Keynes had proposed. Keynes had also urged that Britain arrange normal commercial ties between Russia and Germany, since he thought the above proposals would benefit the British economy. Lenin agreed, and even suggested that the Communist International send a greeting to those economists who were fighting for bolshevism in this manner.

Lenin referred to Keynes on two additional occasions. On December 6, 1920, he delivered the "Speech to the Meeting of the Activists of the Moscow Organization of the RKP."[10] In defending the policy of commercial concessions to foreigners operating in the Soviet Union, he outlined the main reasons for concessions, and maintained that in granting them the Soviet Union would not be at a complete disadvantage and would attempt to exploit the differences and contradictions existing among capitalist nations. He mentioned that America could not reconcile her differences with Europe. "No one has described the Versailles Treaty so well as Keynes, the representative of England to Versailles, did in his book."[11] The world also needed raw materials from Russia, and "Keynes, who wrote *The Economic Consequences of the Peace*, admitted this."[12] Lenin concluded that concessions were necessary. "Concessions— this is not peace with capitalism, but war on a new plane."[13] He admitted that there were dangers in this course but assured the activists that the country would overcome these dangers and emerge stronger economically.

He again mentioned Keynes in his address "On the Internal and Foreign Policy of the Republic,"[14] which he delivered to the Ninth All-Russian Congress of Soviets in Moscow on December 23, 1921. The record revealed that this was Lenin's final reference to Keynes. It is in much the same vein as the previous references. Lenin described the international picture and found that an equilibrium had

10. *Ibid.*, XXXI, 410–429.
11. *Ibid.*, XXXI, 420.
12. *Ibid.*, XXXI, 421.

13. *Ibid.*, XXXI, 428.
14. *Ibid.*, XXXIII, 117–152.

been reached in international relations. This equilibrium, however, contained a high degree of instability. The Soviets, according to him, were better prepared to analyze the contradictions and crises existing in the capitalist countries. He proceeded to quote as an example the financial problems facing the world and noticed that people in the West had begun to change their minds on this topic. He mentioned

the famous writer Keynes, whose book was translated into all languages and who participated in the Versailles negotiations and who placed his entire soul at the service of his government—even he subsequently had to leave it and resign, though still continuing to curse socialism. I repeat that he does not talk and does not even want to think about bolshevism—he tells the capitalist world: What you are doing will lead you into a inescapable position, and then he even advises them simply to cancel all debts.[15]

Since the Soviets had canceled the tsarist debts, Lenin thought it time for the West to follow this example. His analysis continues without further reference to Keynes. Though Lenin agreed with Keynes on the economic difficulties of the treaty, it is clear that each had different hopes regarding the post-treaty world. Lenin wanted the disintegration to continue and agitated for this course, while Keynes wanted to prevent further disaster and wrote his book to this end. Lenin wanted revolution, Keynes desired peace. Lenin stood for the spread of bolshevism, Keynes for the continued existence of capitalism and its institutions in the West, albeit in a modified form. Here, indeed, they were very far apart in their basic positions on the future course of history following the treaty.

However, Lenin's view of Keynes, apart from a few expressions of invective, was relatively favorable in tone. This view was representative of the general attitude toward Keynes prior to the publication of *The General Theory*. This may be substantiated by reference to the entry on Keynes in the first edition of the *Bolshaya Sovetskaya Entsiklopediya* in 1936. This article, written prior to *The General Theory*, is translated and quoted in its entirety:

KEINS (Keynes), John Maynard (b. 1883). Famous English economist, professor of Cambridge University, editor of the *Economic Journal*.

15. *Ibid.*, XXXIII, 120.

Was the representative of the British Treasury to the Versailles peace conference in 1919. Sharply criticized the Versailles Treaty, demonstrating its economic impracticability (particularly the German reparations). "No one has described the Versailles Treaty as well as Keynes did in his book" (Lenin, *Works*, Vol. 25, p. 506). Keynes is an advocate of the quantity theory of money; economic crisis from Keynes's viewpoint can be overcome by means of the regulation of the currency (managed currency). He considered the re-establishment of the gold standard by Churchill, the Minister of Finance, as the source of the economic difficulties of England. With several reservations, he holds to the views of Malthus. Keynes is the chairman of a large English insurance company.

Main works: Indian currency and finance, L., 1913; The economic consequences of the peace, L. 1919 (Russian translation: Ekonomicheskie posledstviya Versalskogo mira, M., 1922); A revision of the treaty, L., 1922 (Russian translation: Peresmotr mirnogo dogovora, M., 1922); A tract on monetary reform, L., 1923 (Russian translation: Traktat o denezhnoi reforme, M., 1925); A short view of Russia, L., 1925; The end of Laissez-faire, L., 1926; A treatise on money, L., 1929; Essays in persuasion [*sic*], 1931.[16]

Apart from the reference to Lenin, there is nothing to distinguish the entry in the Soviet encyclopedia from one to be found in a standard Western reference work of the period. Indeed, one would find it difficult to believe that this was a Soviet source when one compares it with the entry in the second edition of 1953. The first sentence is sufficient to show the striking contrast.

Keynes, John Maynard (1883–1946)—English vulgar bourgeois economist, ideologist of imperialistic reaction and wars, unmasked by V. I. Lenin in 1920 as an avowed bourgeois, a ruthless opponent of bolshevism, which he, as an English philistine, pictures in an ugly, savage, and brutal manner. (*Works*, 4th ed., Vol. 31, p. 195).[17]

Lenin's reference to Keynes as a determined opponent of bolshevism was not quoted out of its context during the period under review. However, in later periods this reference, divorced from its originally more favorable context, was found to be the standard in-

16. *Bolshaya Sovetskaya Entsiklopediya*, 1st ed.; XXXII (Moskva, 1936), 142.
17. *Bolshaya Sovetskaya Entsiklopediya*, 2nd ed.; XX (Moskva, 1953), 488. It is interesting to note that this edition failed to mention any of Keynes's works other than *The General Theory*.

troduction to any mention of Keynes in Soviet economic works. As late as 1958 the *Concise Economic Dictionary* contained the following reference to Keynes: "The class essence of Keynes's position was exhaustively uncovered by Lenin by 1920. According to Lenin's evaluation, Keynes was 'an avowed bourgeois, a ruthless opponent of bolshevism, which he, as an English philistine, pictures in an ugly, savage, and brutal manner' (V. I. Lenin, *Works*, Vol. 31, p. 195)."[18]

A stream of examples might be cited where Soviet writers refer to Keynes, as Lenin did, as an opponent of bolshevism; Lenin, however, also recognized Keynes's ability to see and analyze the consequences of the peace. The majority of references made during the twenties usually cited Keynes only in connection with the economic crisis.

The general index of the Lenin State Library lists the following information on Russian translations of Keynes's early works. *The Economic Consequences of the Peace* was translated into Russian in 1922 and a second edition appeared in 1924. Both editions carried a preface by Sh. M. Dvoilatskii.[19] *A Revision of the Treaty* was translated in 1922 and a second edition appeared in 1924. *The Economic Consequences of Mr. Churchill* was translated into Russian in 1925, with a preface by G. I. Lomov.

When Lenin's speeches were printed in *Pravda*, page references to Keynes's book were not given. His report to the Communist International on July 19, 1920, in Petrograd served as the model of several other reports during this period. A pamphlet by E. Varga and Leon Trotsky described the international situation in terms and language very similar to Lenin's, but contained no references to Keynes.[20] However, both Varga and Trotsky subsequently referred to Keynes in separate works.

In particular, Trotsky referred to Keynes in describing the inter-

18. G. A. Kozlov, S. P. Pervushin, eds., *Kratkii ekonomicheskii slovar* (Moskva, 1958), pp. 122–123.

19. An authorized Russian translation of *The Economic Consequences of the Peace* was published in Stockholm, hence not under Soviet auspices. This was G. P. Struve, T. S. Lure, trans., *Ekonomicheskie posledstviya mira* (Stockholm, 1921).

20. E. Varga and Leon Trotsky, *The International Situation and Our Problems* (Moscow, 1921).

national situation in his famous "Report on the World Economic
Crisis and New Tasks of the Communist International" to the Third
Congress of the Communist International on June 23, 1921.[21] In
the section on international relations, Trotsky dealt with the disintegration of Europe following World War I in these terms:

What caused the war? It was caused as a result of productive forces
being tightly constrained within the boundaries of the most powerful capitalist states. The driving urge of imperialist capital was to abolish borders
and seize the whole world for itself, to abolish customs and boundaries
that were hindering the development of productive forces. In this economic base of imperialism are the reasons for the war. And the results? Europe
is now richer in boundaries and customs than she ever was. A series of
small states have been formed. In the place of former Austro-Hungary,
there are about ten customs boundaries. The Englishman Keynes called
Europe an insane asylum, and in reality, from the point of view of economic development, all this fragmentation into small states with their
tight customs systems and so forth demonstrates a weird anachronism, a
mad intrusion of the Middle Ages into the twentieth century. At the same
time that the Balkan peninsula is becoming barbarianized, Europe is becoming Balkanized.[22]

After the name "Keynes" in the above text, there was a footnote
reference in which Trotsky gave the following information on
Keynes:

242. *Keynes*—a most prominent English economist. After the war he
was a member of the Supreme Economic Council of the Entente. In a
series of works Keynes demonstrated the economic senselessness of the
Versailles Treaty and predicted back in 1919 the fruitless decisions of
Versailles. Here we have in mind his first work, *The Economic Consequences of the Peace*.[23]

This was not the only reference that Trotsky made to Keynes.
During the two-hundredth anniversary celebrations of the founding
of the Russian Academy of Sciences, Trotsky addressed the Fourth
Mendeleev Congress for Pure and Applied Chemistry on September
17, 1925, on the subject of "D. I. Mendeleev and Marxism."[24] He
discussed Mendeleev's view of Malthus, saying that Mendeleev, in

21. L. Trotskii, *Pyat let kominterna* (Moskva, 1924), pp. 138–196.
22. *Ibid.*, pp. 176–177.   23. *Ibid.*, p. 600.
24. L. Trotskii, *Sochineniya*, XXI (Moskva, 1927), 268–288.

his day (1906), had refused to be concerned even if there were to be ten billion people within one hundred and fifty to two hundred years because science in the future would find the means of subsistence for even more people if necessary. At this point of the address, Trotsky referred to Keynes:

The current advice the English professor Keynes offered at these academic celebrations, which concerned the limiting of the growth of population, would not have met with the least sympathy from our great chemist and industrial optimist. Dmitrii Ivanovich [Mendeleev] would have only repeated his own old words: "Do not these new Malthusians wish to stop this growth? In my opinion, the more crowded we are the cosier it will be."[25]

The above reference to Keynes was annotated as follows:

No. 91—*Professor Keynes*—outstanding English economist; delivered a report on the economic situation in England to the plenum of the Industrial Economic Council of the Supreme Soviet of the National Economy on 14 September 1925. In his report Keynes explained that the main reason for unemployment in England was that the growth of the working force greatly exceeded its natural decrease. On the subject of unemployment in the USSR, Prof. Keynes expressed the matter in this manner:

"I assume that the poverty of prewar Russia occurred to a considerable degree because of the exceptional increase in population. Again at the present time one notices an increase in the birth rate over the death rate. For the economic future of Russia—this is the very greatest danger. One of the most important questions of state policy is the achievement of a relationship between the growth of the population and the development of the productive forces of the country" (*Economicheskaya Zhizn*, No. 210, 15 September 1925).[26]

Trotsky found fault with Keynes's analysis and warned the scientists against applying the laws of a particular physical science to the study of a social science. Confusion resulted, Trotsky continued, when this incorrect line was taken, as was the case with Malthus and Keynes. He assured the assembly that population would be no problem for the Soviet Union as it had correctly understood these lessons. However, population and unemployment remained a problem for England, and though she had achieved industrialization, she

25. *Ibid.*, XXI, 284.   26. *Ibid.*, XXI, 495.

had to resort to emigration to seek relief from this problem. "Even the most 'progressive' economist Keynes only a few days ago reported to us that the salvation of the English economy—was in Malthusianism!"[27] Trotsky, it is evident, was up to date on Keynes's activities. It is interesting to note that Sir Roy Harrod, Keynes's chief biographer, sketched this Russian visit by Keynes in less than one-half page and made no mention of Keynes's lecture to the Supreme Economic Council.[28]

The following year Keynes reviewed Trotsky's book *Where Is England Going?*[29] Keynes's criticisms bring into sharp relief the essential differences between his views of the future and Trotsky's. Of Trotsky's book he says: "Its dogmatic tone about our affairs, where even the author's flashes of insight are clouded by his inevitable ignorance of what he is talking about, cannot commend it to an English reader."[30] He saw the essence of Trotsky's message as an attack on the British Labour party for attempting to gain socialism without revolution. In dealing with Trotsky's propositions on the historical process, Keynes found them to be logical but based on faulty assumptions, namely, "that the moral and intellectual problems of the transformation of Society have been already solved—that a plan exists, and that nothing remains except to put it into operation."[31] Keynes ended with an appeal for the use of reason to solve human problems and with an indictment of the utter uselessness of force, the doctrine of Trotsky. "The next move," Keynes concluded, "is with the head, and fists must wait."[32]

No direct reference to Keynes was found in Stalin's works. Perhaps this is due to the nature of Stalin's speeches and writings. When speaking on the international situation, Stalin expressed himself in very general terms. His style was simpler and more direct than that of Lenin or Trotsky. His speeches contained few references to anyone except Marx or Lenin, or his own immediate opponents. In dealing with economic crises, he was to set a pattern that became

27. *Ibid.*, XXI, 286.
28. Roy F. Harrod, *The Life of John Maynard Keynes* (New York, 1951), p. 365.
29. London, 1926. The Russian edition was *Kuda idyot Angliya?* (Moskva, 1925).
30. J. M. Keynes, "Trotsky on England," *The Nation and the Athenæum*, XXXVIII (March 27, 1926), 884.
31. *Ibid.*, p. 885.   32. *Ibid.*

very familiar in later years. An example of his "roving" analysis is taken from the "Political Report of the Central Committee to the Sixteenth Congress of the CPSU,"[33] which he gave on June 27, 1930.

The most diverse "theories" about crises are being invented. Whole schemes are being proposed for "mitigating," "preventing," and "eliminating" crises. The bourgeois oppositions are blaming the bourgeois governments because "they failed to take all measures" to prevent the crisis . . . . There are even wiseacres who ascribed the world economic crisis to the "machinations of the Bolsheviks."

It goes without saying that none of these "theories" and schemes has anything in common with science. It must be admitted that the bourgeois economists have proved to be utter bankrupts in the face of the crisis. More than that, they have been found to be devoid even of that little sense of reality which their predecessors could not always be said to lack.[34]

In this report Stalin also discussed the reparations problem. He concluded, as Keynes had earlier, that Germany would not be able to pay the indemnities, and added that the German proletariat would not allow itself to be exploited by the victorious powers. Keynes had thought that the governments were committing madness to enforce the treaty. Stalin likewise thought that the politicians were out of their minds if they believed that the German proletariat would pay the reparations without a struggle.[35] Such are the similarities between Stalin and Keynes on the consequences of the peace, though Stalin made no acknowledgment or reference to Keynes's thought.

Soviet economists were beginning to take note of Keynes's growing influence and standing in the West. N. N. Lyubimov and A. N. Erlikh were Russian representatives at the Genoa Conference in 1922,[36] and their later recollections of the political atmosphere of those days is revealing:

In Germany, businessmen and politicans were racking their brains over the reparations tangle produced by Versailles. Large-scale unemployment and falling trade with Europe and other parts of the world were pushing up the political temperature in Britain, where the economist John May-

33. J. V. Stalin, *Works*, XII (Moscow, 1955), 242–385.
34. *Ibid.*, XII, 249–250.   35. *Ibid.*, XII, 257.
36. This was a conference on economic affairs concerning the reconstruction of Central and Eastern Europe. The main issues were those of the Russian debts and the compensation for loss of foreign property in Soviet Russia.

nard Keynes was demanding a review of the entire reparations system and urging a compromise with Soviet Russia.[37]

Chicherin, the head of the Russian delegation at Genoa, saw a notice of Keynes's new book, *A Revision of the Treaty*, and wondered if this was the work which Comrade Lenin had mentioned. He ordered the book to be purchased locally if possible, and if not, that arrangements be made to buy it in Berlin on the return journey.[38]

Academician E. V. Tarle in a standard work of the period discussed the secrecy surrounding the leaders of the victorious powers at Versailles. This secrecy would have been complete, according to the Soviet historian had it not been for "indiscretions" from Keynes and others close to the Big Four.[39] Another reference to Keynes was found in an early work by Academician E. Varga, one of the foremost Soviet economists throughout the history of the Soviet Union. Varga referred to Keynes's estimate of Marxism with these words: "Another luminary of present-day bourgeois economics, Keynes, regards Marxism with the helplessness of a child."[40]

Despite his extremely active role in the hotly debated economic issues of his own country, Keynes found time to visit Russia twice, to write several short works on the Soviet Union, and to comment frequently on the progress and the nature of the Soviet economy. However, Harrod's biography has little to say on his standing in Soviet Russia for the relevant period. As we have noted, Keynes's major works during this period were listed in the first edition of the Russian encyclopedia, and several of his works were translated into Russian. Very little comment was found on Keynes's works other than *The Economic Consequences of the Peace*. In view of his frequent comments on Soviet affairs, it is surprising that there was not a wider mention of him by the Soviets during this period.

Broadly speaking, the Soviets viewed Keynes more favorably in this period than in any other because he had not yet been identified as their main opponent in the field of economics. This is not alto-

---

37. N. N. Lyubimov and A. N. Erlikh, "The 1922 Genoa Conference," *International Affairs* (Moscow), 1963, No. 6, p. 65.
38. N. N. Lyubimov and A. N. Erlikh, *International Affairs*, 1963, No. 10, p. 77.
39. E. V. Tarle, *Europa v epokhu imperializma* (Moskva, 1927), p. 430.
40. E. Varga, *The Decline of Capitalism* (London, 1928), p. 15.

gether surprising, as *The General Theory* had not yet appeared. Also, Keynes's highly critical view of the Versailles Treaty and his attitude toward reparations were very acceptable to the Soviets. At this time certain of his criticisms of the post-World War I period could be conveniently turned as arguments against the capitalist system in the world. It is evident that Keynes was respected and recognized in the Soviet Union for his penetrating analysis of the then current economic problems even before the appearance of *The General Theory*.

III. *The Soviet position on Keynes 1936-1948*

The appearance of *The General Theory* in 1936 seems to have been simply ignored for a couple of years in the Soviet Union. A review of the economic publications of the period reveals no mention of it until 1938.[1] This is less surprising when one reflects that at the time of its publication it received neither an auspicious nor a cordial welcome by its reviewers in the West. "Not a single enthusiastic review has come to my attention; and there were many very critical ones," Seymour Harris was to note.[2] Keynes and his theory were not even mentioned in the presidential address by Professor Alvin Johnson delivered in Chicago at the meeting of the American Economic Association on December 29, 1936, in which Johnson appealed to economists "to organize themselves effectively to do the work which society may reasonably require of them."[3] Another probable reason for the neglect of Keynes's work by the Soviets is that no translation of it was made until 1948, and the work is by no means easy reading even for one fluent in English.

A review of the relevant journals and economic texts during the beginning of this period reveals that Soviet writers were still referring to Keynes but not to *The General Theory*. Academician E. Varga in his article "The End of the Gold Bloc and the Currency Problem in the Period of the General Crisis"[4] still thought of Keynes principally as the author of *A Treatise on Money*. According to

---

1. This writer of course does not claim to have exhausted the literature for the period under review. However, an attempt has been made to survey the available materials, in particular the relevant issues of the principal Soviet political and economic journals, *Bolshevik, Planovoe Khozaistvo, Problemy Ekonomiki,* and *Mirovoe Khozyaistvo i Mirovaya Politika.*
2. Seymour E. Harris, ed., *The New Economics* (New York, 1950), p. 29.
3. Alvin Johnson, "The Economist in a World in Transition," *American Economic Review*, XXVII (March, 1937), 3.
4. E. Varga, "Konets zolotogo bloka i valyutnaya problema v period obshchego krizisa," *Mirovoe Khozyaistvo i Mirovaya Politika*, 1936, No. 11, pp. 17–30.

Varga: "The theory of Keynes and company that the crisis of capitalism can be overcome by the 'manipulation' of the currency and interest rates, the theory which thanks to the 'co-operation' of de Man has penetrated fairly deeply in social-democratic circles is vulgar, superficial, and false."[5] The capitalist countries, Varga contended, could not solve their problems by currency manipulations, as artificial interference in the area of exchange could not affect production but only modify it to an insignificant degree.

Likewise we find another Soviet economist, Professor Z. Atlas, in a review of Vygodskii's book *Credit and Credit Policy in the U.S.A.*,[6] mentioning Keynes's *A Treatise on Money*. In this book "certain bourgeois economists, despite the stock exchange collapse which occurred in 1929, continued to praise this policy [Federal Reserve Open Market Operations] seeing in it a 'triumph' of the ideas of regulation."[7] A long quote from *A Treatise on Money* followed to show that the Federal Reserve's management of the dollar from 1923 to 1928 was a triumph despite the weakening events of 1929–1930, because, according to Keynes, it demonstrated that management by means of currency circulation was possible.

The world economic crisis was given particular emphasis by the Soviet writers of this period, but no notice seems to have been taken of *The General Theory* until 1938. Strangely, even Keynes's articles entitled "How We Can Avoid a Slump," which appeared in the London *Times* of January 12, 13, and 14, 1937, received brief comment before any reference was found to *The General Theory*. According to the Soviets, these articles demonstrated the uncertainties among English economists as England was approaching a new crisis.[8] On the subject of economic crisis, Varga in 1938 still found Western economic science wanting in regard to solving the existing crisis:

Bourgeois economic science up to this time has not understood or has not wanted to give an explanation as to why general crises of overproduc-

5. *Ibid.*, p. 30.
6. Z. Atlas, review of S. Vygodskii, *Kredit i kreditnaya politika v SShA* (Moskva, 1936), *Planovoe Khozyaistvo*, 1937, No. 2, pp. 172–175.
7. *Ibid.*, p. 173.
8. E. Varga, ed., *Mirovoe khozyaistvo v 1936g* (Moskva, 1937), p. 218.

tion are inevitable under capitalism. The argument of bourgeois science at the present differs in no way from the argument it gave 110 years ago. The new books of the bourgeois economists on the questions of the cycles, the crises, and the conditions of the capitalist economy are evidence of this. One can assume that everything continues in the old way with them; nothing has changed in bourgeois discussions on the reasons for crises; and bourgeois theoretical economics does not give any new arguments.[9]

But facts are facts, continued Varga, and they must be explained. He mentioned two schools that attempted to deal with crises in the West. One school, which he attributed to Kautsky, Hilferding, Bukharin, and Otto Bauer, was composed of adherents of the theory of proportions. The other school believed in the insufficiency of loan capital; this he called the school of Keynes and Wicksell. Thus at this time the leading Soviet authority on world economic problems and a constant and voluminous contributor to all the relevant journals had failed to deal with or even mention *The General Theory*, which was certainly a noteworthy attempt from the West to come to grips with the economic crisis at hand.

The first mention of *The General Theory* is found in an article by L. Freiman on "Unemployment in the Capitalist Countries."[10] Freiman concentrated on unemployment problems and the attempts to solve them. His thesis ran along these lines:

The bourgeois economists make every effort to conceal the special character of unemployment in the period of the general crisis of capitalism. In fulfilling the social commands of the capitalistic class, the most prominent bourgeois economists attempt to prove "scientifically" that unemployment can be overcome within the framework of capitalist society. Thus the famous English economist Keynes in his voluminous work entitled *The General Theory of Employment, Interest and Money* came to the conclusion that to gather all the working force into production it is necessary to increase investment and the personal consumption of the members of society. In his opinion, this growth of investment can be achieved by means of lowering the interest rate or something that Keynes

9. E. Varga, "Ekonomicheskii krizis v SShA predvestnik novogo mirovogo ekonomicheskogo krizisa," *Mirovoe Khozyaistvo i Mirovaya Politika*, 1938, No. 1, p. 11.

10. L. Freiman, "Bezrabotitsa v kapitalisticheskikh stranakh," *Planovoe Khozyaistvo*, 1938, No. 8, pp. 106–120.

thinks has a greater chance for realization—the creation of state projects. The state, which has the power of intervention, must act to increase personal consumption by such measures (taxes, social services and others) as would guarantee the redistribution of income among the different sections of the population.

One should not say that the conclusions of Keynes are a novelty. Analogous repair patches on capitalism were offered by reformers of various creeds in the USA and other countries long ago. Economic reality has proved the unadaptability of all these prescriptions for the saving of the capitalist system a countless number of times. The deep economic cyclical crisis is deepening all the more at the present time in the USA. Tied to this crisis is the further massive growth of unemployment that is occurring with the presence of the *exceptionally low* level of the *discount rate and despite* widespread distribution of state projects.[11]

Freiman, in footnotes to the above paragraphs, referred to the 1 per cent discount rate of the Federal Reserve Bank in effect during September, 1937, and the Senate approval of a $3.7 billion dollar unemployment measure in June, 1938, as measures failing to stem unemployment. He maintained that Keynes had received a sharp rebuke from Cassel, another pillar of bourgeois economic science. However, Cassel's criticisms of Keynes were not reviewed very sympathetically by Freiman. He found Cassel "a zealous apologist of capitalism who has not forgotten about his old theories on 'equilibrium' of the national economy and has learnt nothing from observation of the new features in the development of capitalism in the postwar years and considers that capitalism does not need any sort of artificial measures."[12] Freiman quoted Cassel as perhaps applying Keynesian measures only in an economy suffering from complete economic paralysis. According to Freiman, Cassel considered Keynes's theory "a declaration of war" on saving and "hastens to assure his bourgeois readers that the results of the investigation by Keynes cannot in any case be viewed as the 'last word of economic science.' "[13] Freiman continued to examine critically Cassel's ideas, but there were no references to any of Cassel's works. In Freiman's discussion of Keynes, there were no references to any

11. *Ibid.*, p. 107.
12. *Ibid.*

13. *Ibid.*, p. 108.

pages in *The General Theory*, but the English title was given in a footnote without any further information. Hence the Russian reader would not know the publisher or the date or place of publication. However, the article did at least give the reader a general idea of Keynes's theories and presented him in a more favorable light than Cassel. The remainder of the article surveyed the employment picture of the leading nations and was full of statistics that vividly portrayed the existence of heavy unemployment everywhere. The conclusion stressed the hopelessness of attempting to solve this problem within the capitalistic framework and asserted that economic reality had obviously demonstrated this.

Articles continued to appear in the late thirties without reference to *The General Theory*. For example, P. Polyak, in a survey article entitled "The Economic Crisis in England,"[14] failed to mention Keynes at all. Polyak reviewed the economic position of England and only had this to say regarding economists: "Bourgeois economists and prominent English capitalists in their 'analysis' of the economic position of England place the blame for the present crisis, or as they say, depression, on the USA, where the beginning of the crisis led to the worsening of the economic situation in England."[15]

Toward the end of the thirties, mention of Keynes and of *The General Theory* was found in a number of book reviews. S. Goldin's review of the Western economist Jurgen Kuczynski's *New Fashions in Wage Theory* was the first account to be found that mentioned Keynes in connection with wages.[16] Goldin, who classified Kuczynski as an anti-fascist economist, approved of his critical treatment and interpretation of Keynes, about whom Goldin says the following in his review:

Keynes is also for the reduction of wages, but he approaches it from the other end. He attempts to conceal the lowering of wages and shows a means of reducing the living standard of the workers that would be difficult for them to detect and that would weaken their opposition to the encroachment by the capitalists.

14. P. Polyak, "Ekonomicheskii krizis v Anglii," *Planovoe Khozyaistvo*, 1938, No. 9, pp. 129–142.
15. *Ibid.*, p. 133.
16. S. Goldin, review of Jurgen Kuczynski, *New Fashions in Wage Theory* (London, 1937), *Planovoe Khozyaistvo*, 1938, No. 12, pp. 182–184.

Keynes considers that the reason for crises is the factual or expected fall of the "marginal efficiency of capital." Against this fall of the "effectiveness of capital" is one basic remedy—the lowering of interest on loans accompanied by an increase in prices. In this way it is possible, in the opinion of Keynes, to direct and to control investment in a manner that would react on the entire economy: production, employment, and so forth.

Proceeding from this theory, Keynes calls for the "stabilization" of money wages, but at the same time he defends the lowering of real wages by means of increasing prices.

The realization of these measures he entrusts to the state, which will introduce them in a "planned" manner, increasing the profits of the capitalists, lowering the living level of the workers, and intensifying their exploitation.[17]

This distorted interpretation of Keynes on wages became the standard for future references on this subject. In reality Keynes favored a stabilized wage policy in the short run but rising wages with stable prices in the long run.[18] In Goldin's review, even though investment was mentioned as the main cause for crises, the subject of wages was given overwhelming significance. Nevertheless, Goldin did consider Keynes's work of sufficient value to merit the following recommendation: "This book undoubtedly deserves the attention of the Soviet reader."[19]

Another Soviet authority, Professor I. G. Blyumin of Moscow University, made a passing reference to *The General Theory* in reviewing Erich Roll's *A History of Economic Thought*.[20] Blyumin was one of the chief Soviet experts on Western economic thought from the twenties until his death in 1959. This appears to be his earliest reference to Keynes. He was concerned with the question of the membership and true descendants of the classical school in economics. He maintained that vulgar bourgeois economists had tried to break the connection between the English classical school and Marx. In his view, these bourgeois economists had attempted to interpret Smith and Ricardo in their own vulgar image and separate

17. *Ibid.*, p. 183.
18. Keynes, *The General Theory*, pp. 270–271.
19. Goldin, p. 184.
20. I. Blyumin, review of Erich Roll, *A History of Economic Thought* (London, 1938), *Problemy Ekonomiki*, 1939, No. 5, pp. 203–206.

them from the labor theory of value. Blyumin claimed this tendency to be increasing. "For example, Keynes in his sensational book *The General Theory of Employment, Interest and Money* includes such vulgarizers and apologists of capitalism as Marshall. The classical school in the opinion of Keynes, exists in England at the present in the personage of Pigou—the most prominent representative of contemporary vulgar economics in England."[21] According to Blyumin, Roll presented the correct view in considering J. S. Mill as the last of the classical school and was absolutely correct in including the labor theory of value as an organic part of this school's teachings.

Prior to the Soviet entry into World War II, an article by A. Arutinyan on "The Harvard Economists and Bourgeois Economic Observations" dealt with Mitchell and Keynes.[22] This article was prepared as a chapter for a book on the history of economic thought to be published by the Institute of Economics of the Academy of Sciences. Although the article placed Mitchell and Keynes on equal footing, Mitchell received greater attention and criticism. Arutinyan did make the distinction that Mitchell's work dealt with the cyclical movement of capitalist production whereas Keynes's was an attempt to solve crises.[23]

Although Keynes was not a Harvard economist, Arutinyan included a brief summary of *The General Theory* in his article. The problem and danger to capitalism was unemployment, and Keynes, in his view, had attempted to solve this problem. Arutinyan described the role of consumption and investment in *The General Theory* with emphasis on increasing both components:

> In contemporary circumstances this falls on the shoulders of the state, which should increase unproductive consumption (from this flows the apologetics of militarism and imperialist war), widen the investment in organizations for social works, and lower the rate of interest with the goal of driving it to zero.[24]

Arutinyan claimed that Keynes's theory was a mixture of the bankrupt ideas of Malthus regarding unproductive consumption and the Austrian school of political economy regarding marginal productiv-

21. *Ibid.*, p. 204.
22. A. Arutinyan, "Garvardskie ekonomisty i burzhuaznoe konyunkturovedenie," *Problemy Ekonomiki*, 1940, No. 9, pp. 151–165.
23. *Ibid.*, p. 151.   24. *Ibid.*, p. 165.

ity. The above ideas were bagged together with a lot of demagoguery about unemployment and the role of the state. "This theory is one of the many attempts of bourgeois economic science to adapt its apologetics to the demands of the rule of capital at the present stage of development."[25]

With the advent of World War II, references to *The General Theory* became increasingly rare. Still no formal review of *The General Theory* was found. However, mention of Keynes appeared in the Soviet literature, but in the context of the economic problems arising from the war. His book *How to Pay for the War*[26] was reviewed in the journals and received widespread adverse comment. It appears that the Soviets, increasingly aware of Keynes, noticed his efforts to help the British economy during this period.

In 1938 Keynes contributed an article to *The Economic Journal* on problems of raw materials.[27] This was one of the main sources for an article by S. Vishnev in 1940 on state reserves in the capitalist countries.[28] Vishnev found the foreign literature very slender on this subject and maintained that "the works of the German, Professor Gaebel, and the famous English economist, Keynes, deserve attention. In these works there are not only theoretical conceptions but also more concrete, practical proposals, which have been put into practice in one form or another."[29] Vishnev outlined the similarities of each plan and then proceeded to give sympathetic emphasis to their differences. He especially noticed the further possibilities of Keynes's plan:

Thus, just as Gaebel did, Keynes noticed that money reserves, resources in money form, in conditions of war will not easily be accepted as payment. It would be safer to have reserves in their natural form and not somewhere in the dominions and colonies but at home on English soil. He even considers that reserves of goods are preferable to gold reserves. At the same time the conclusions of Keynes differ from Gaebel's, and the essence of Keynes's conception is that state reserves are not only viewed

25. *Ibid.*   26. London, 1940.

27. J. M. Keynes, "The Policy of Government Storage of Foodstuffs and Raw Materials," *The Economic Journal*, XLVIII (Sept., 1938), 449–460.

28. S. Vishnev, "Gosudarstvennye reservy v kapitalisticheskikh stranakh," *Planovoe Khozyaistvo*, 1940, No. 10, pp. 84–94.

29. *Ibid.*, p. 86.

as an indirect fund but as maneuverable resources to act on the economic situation. The direction of the state reserves, according to Keynes, will not only be against the blockade but also against the instability and the cycles of the capitalist economy.

Moreover, Keynes thoroughly justifies the economic expediency of the creation of such reserves. He maintains in particular that the purchases of raw materials and foodstuffs for reserves in England will stimulate English exports to those countries where these purchases were produced. Further, he notices that the appearance of such reserves on English territory is the best guarantee for English investment overseas . . . .[30]

Vishnev did not offer any serious objection to Keynes's plan. He noticed that Keynes's ideas "found a favorable response among English and American economists."[31] In fact, Vishnev not only refrained from criticizing the above plans but recommended his readers to study the experience and the techniques of the foreigners in these matters. Perhaps as a necessary afterthoughts, he concluded that by understanding the supply and reserve position of the capitalist countries, one would be able to evaluate correctly the "imperialist coalition" and its fight to redivide the world.[32]

Not everyone was so favorably disposed toward Keynes. One writer, A. Grigorev, discussed labor mobilization in the capitalist countries.[33] In his comments on an article by Makower and Robinson that had appeared in *The Economic Journal*,[34] he even took Keynes to task for being the editor! Makower and Robinson had examined the problem of mobilizing labor reserves. In their analysis they had counted on the market mechanism to distribute labor. Grigorev, with the advantage of two years' hindsight, was able to see their mistakes and consequently the necessary mobilization schemes that followed. He commented that "reality proved more complex than expected for Keynes and the authors of the journal of the Royal Economic Society, the authoritative organ of bourgeois political economy."[35] Workers, Grigorev predicted, would not stand

30. *Ibid.*, p. 87.
31. *Ibid.*, p. 88.   32. *Ibid.*, p. 94.
33. A. Grigorev, "Voina i mobilizatsiya truda v stranakh kapitala," *Planovoe Khozyaistvo*, 1941, No. 1, pp. 64–78.
34. H. Makower and H. W. Robinson, "Labour Potential in War-Time," *The Economic Journal*, XLIX (Dec., 1939), 624–640.
35. Grigorev, p. 66.

for unemployment and hunger in peacetime and forced labor in wartime.

An article by L. Geller, "The Working Class of the Capitalist Countries After Five Months of War in Europe," discussed Keynes's proposals to finance the war.[36] Geller did not cite any source for his references to Keynes other than this mystifying sentence: "On the pages of the semi-official organ of the City of London there appeared an article by Keynes that attracted great attention and that was devoted to the question of how best to limit the underconsumption of the workers."[37] Geller claimed that Keynes had wanted to lower the real wages of the workers by 10 per cent. Since rationing was ineffective, Keynes had opted for forced saving, which would be returned to the workers after the war. The trade-union leaders had compromised the workers by their policy of co-operation with the government. The English Communist party had exposed Keynes's plan as it was directed only against the workers. In Geller's opinion, Keynes's plan had little chance of success.

Reviewing Keynes's *How to Pay for the War*,[38] Academician Varga restated the problem facing Keynes in this manner: "how best to satisfy the needs of the army and the war, and yet to avert inflation and not to arouse the dangerous dissatisfaction of the proletariat."[39] By including the proletariat in the problem, Varga proceeded to concentrate on this issue and interpreted *How to Pay for the War* from this angle. To his credit, he recognized the essentials of Keynes's plan but detected a strong anti-worker bias. "The anti-worker character of the plan is most clearly revealed in that chapter in which the author attempts to prove that *the expense of the war in no way can be covered by the rich*."[40] Keynes's table on income groups on page 22 is reproduced by Varga, but the footnote stating

36. L. Geller, "Rabochii klass kapitalisticheskikh stran posle pyati mesyatsev voiny v Evrope," *Mirovoe Khozyaistvo i Mirovaya Politika,* 1940, No. 1, pp. 61–80.
37. *Ibid.,* p. 70. This reference was probably to one of a series of Keynes's articles on paying for the war, which appeared in *The Times* on Nov. 14, 15, and 28, 1939.
38. E. Varga, review of J. M. Keynes, *How to Pay for the War* (London, 1940), *Mirovoe Khozyaistvo i Mirovaya Politika*, 1940, No. 6, pp. 200–202.
39. *Ibid.,* p. 200.
40. *Ibid.,* p. 201. Here Varga has in mind chap. iv, entitled "Can the Rich Pay for the War?"

that these were prewar classifications was conveniently omitted. Varga dismissed the entrepreneur incentive argument and stoutly maintained that the rich could pay for the war:

All this argumentation by Keynes cannot stand up to criticism. Of course the rich class in the population can cover the expenses of the war in the *form of money*, and if not completely from their current income, then in any case from their capital. No matter how Keynes attempts to convince the workers to accept his plan voluntarily, though he may be successful in persuading the biggest trade-union leaders, he will have no success with the working masses.[41]

Despite his conclusion that the workers would not accept Keynes's plan, Varga found them bearing the burden of the war in England, or in any capitalist country for that matter. He ended with an expression from Lenin that "war is hell for the workers," apparently an extension of the famous remark attributed to General Sherman.

Much the same approach was taken by some individual who signed only his initials to his review of Keynes's book.[42] L. F. stated the essentials of Keynes's position in brief form and then proceeded to attack it in a manner similar to Varga's, that is, from the anti-class point of view. He pointed out that Keynes knew very well that he could count on the trade-union leaders for the greatest support of his plan. L. F. was especially critical of Keynes's idea to postpone a capital levy until after the war:

The class character of Keynes's "plan" is clearly expressed thus: a part of the wages will be paid to the workers after the war, but a part of the tax on the capitalists will be postponed until after the war. Moreover, Keynes considers it necessary to make a reservation, that a capital tax should not necessarily be levied immediately after the war but only when there is an economic recovery. Thus, consistently and carefully Keynes defends the interests of capital.[43]

Again Keynes's plan was not given much chance of success.

Other examples were found in the literature, but they would not

41. *Ibid.*, p. 202.
42. L. F., review of J. M. Keynes, *How to Pay for the War* (London, 1940), *Problemy Ekonomiki*, 1940, No. 9, pp. 172–173. L. F. might have been L. Freiman, who first mentioned *The General Theory* when writing on employment and wage theory.
43. *Ibid.*, p. 173.

be very different in content.[44] I. Sosenskii found that the Americans were following policies similar to the British ones and mentioned the influence of Keynes.[45] With the German invasion of the Soviet Union, references to Keynes's plan ceased. True, many publications were discontinued during these difficult times, but those that kept publishing even on an irregular schedule gave no further attention to Keynes's plan while war was in progress.

How to Pay for the War was thus presented in a distorted way to the Soviet readers. In reality, Keynes considered that he was furthering the best interests of the workers with his plan. He stressed this point time and time again throughout his book. For example:

> By such a plan, as I hope to show, the wage and salary earner can consume as much as before and in addition have money over in the bank for his future benefit and security, which would belong otherwise to the capitalist class.[46]

Again:

> It also means that rights to deferred consumption after the war, which is another name for National Debt, will be widely distributed amongst all those who are foregoing immediate consumption, instead of being mainly concentrated, as they were last time, in the hands of the capitalist class.[47]

And again:

> But we can reward him [the worker] by giving him a share in the claims on the future which would belong otherwise to the entrepreneurs.[48]

Yet Keynes was presented in an entirely different light to the Soviet reader and the book received more attention and comment than *The General Theory* had up to this point.

Toward the end of the war journals resumed regular publication. Still no formal review of *The General Theory* was found by the writer, but Keynes was mentioned, and his participation at the international monetary conferences (Bretton Woods and Savannah)

---

44. For example, S. Lang, "Ekonomicheskoe polozhenie Anglii," *Mirovoe Khozyaistvo i Mirovaya Politika*, 1941, No. 5, pp. 14–26.

45. I. Sosenskii, review of John A. Krout, ed., *The Effect of the War on America's Idle Men and Money* (New York, 1940), *Mirovoe Khozyaistvo i Mirovaya Politika*, 1940, No. 10, pp. 134–135.

46. Keynes, *How to Pay for the War*, p. 5.

47. *Ibid.*, pp. 10–11.   48. *Ibid.*, p. 74.

was discussed. The leading contributor on this role of Keynes was Academician I. A. Trakhtenberg. In an article entitled "The International Monetary Fund and the Bank for Reconstruction and Development,"[49] Trakhtenberg gave his report on these events:

The Conference was preceded by two years of continuous work. Two projects were put forth at the start: the English known under the name of Keynes and the American known under the name of White. Both plans were discussed for the solution of the very same problem, but they differed from each other not only in basic general principles but in the methods of achieving their aims. The differing characteristics of both plans are defined by the special differences and the opposing interests in the relationship between England and the United States.[50]

Trakhtenberg reported that the American plan was largely accepted. Parity was fixed in terms of gold or dollars.

With this decision, the various types of nominalist theories were rejected and the illusions of regulated capitalist currency, independent from gold, were discarded. In this matter the American point of view triumphed completely and the nominalist, quantity theory that was supported by Keynes, the author of the English project, was thrown out.[51]

Trakhtenberg was against the nominalist theory. He did approve, however, of Soviet participation in the conference and said this would strengthen these organizations. He even predicted a prominent role for the bank and the fund in the future.

In another article, "The Projects of the International Monetary Agreements,"[52] Trakhtenberg again reviewed both plans. He outlined England's future trade position, and he accurately predicted that England would have trade difficulties in the future as she would have to export more as a result of her losses on invisible earnings. Hence, he said, credit would be necessary, and Keynes's plan for an International Clearing Union would help provide the credit. Trakhtenberg tied this union to the ideas of Keynes in his *Treatise on Monetary Reform*. After summarizing Keynes's ideas on money,

---

49. I. A. Trakhtenberg, "Mezhdunarodnyi valyutnyi fond i bank dlya rekonstruktsii i razvitiya," *Planovoe Khozyaistvo,* 1944, No. 2, pp. 69–80.
50. *Ibid.,* p. 69. 51. *Ibid.,* p. 72.
52. I. A. Trakhtenberg, "Proekty mezhdunarodnykh valyutnykh soglashenii," *Mirovoe Khozyaistvo i Mirovaya Politika,* 1944, Nos. 1–2, pp. 25–40.

Trakhtenberg rejected them. "It is hardly necessary to prove the incorrectness of these nominalist theories and the illusoriness of the hopes to attain a stable currency by a simple agreement."[53] He also noted that not all Englishmen supported Keynes, and that the gold interests especially opposed him.

Trakhtenberg commented again on the above projects in his book *The Financial Results of the War*, which appeared early in 1946.[54] He referred to Keynes several times in this book, discussing his work at the Treasury during World War I and commending him for his analysis of the financial difficulties ahead for Great Britain. In this context Lloyd George was taken to task. Keynes's *Treatise on Monetary Reform* was discussed at length. Keynes's plan at Bretton Woods was given much the same treatment as it had received in the above-mentioned articles. *The General Theory* was not mentioned in any of the above sources. In the conclusions to his book, Trakhtenberg admitted to the possibility of a solution of the currency difficulties in the capitalist countries. Since the book was sent to the publisher in June, 1945, perhaps this conclusion can be attributed to a wartime spirit of co-operation. It was, however, encouraging to read:

But at the same time, the given example shows that despite those contradictions acceptable decisions can be found. The entire capitalistic world is interested in stable currency; therefore the solving of the currency problem is possible within the framework of capitalism on the condition of overcoming the resistance of the reactionary elements that in our time are the carriers of fascist ideas.[55]

In the early postwar period there were increasingly frequent and varied references to Keynes in Soviet sources. Professor P. Maslov noted that Keynes had sharpened the problem of probability with his critique.[56] Another reviewer, A. Gusakov, found lack of mention of Keynes to be the one serious omission in F. I. Mikhalevskii's *Gold in the Period of the World Wars*:

53. *Ibid.*, p. 31.
54. *Finansovye itogi voiny* (Moskva, 1946).
55. *Ibid.*, p. 102.
56. P. P. Maslov, review of Academician V. S. Nemchinov, *Selskhozyaistvennaya statistika s osnovami obshchei teorii* (Moskva, 1945), *Izvestiya Akademii Nauk SSSR*, Otdelenie Ekonomiki i Prava, 1946, No. 3, p. 262.

It should be observed that if the author gave comparatively much attention to the anti-gold demagogues of the German fascists and gave them appropriate criticism, then the question of nominalist conceptions in other countries, especially in Britain, where they are now receiving exceptionally wide distribution, is touched on only lightly. It would have been especially fitting to give Keynes's point of view on gold already developed by him in the twenties and later [here a footnote reference to *The General Theory* is given] and again its expression and further development in the stabilization of the currency in the postwar period proposed by the English delegation at the International Monetary Conference at Bretton Woods.[57]

In a book review entitled "The False Prophet Keynes,"[58] Academician Varga reviewed E. Mantoux's *The Carthaginian Peace— or The Economic Consequences of Mr. Keynes*. Mantoux, it will be recalled, stated the case against Keynes's evaluation of the Versailles Treaty. Varga took issue with Mantoux and defended Keynes by saying that he had been instrumental in calling the treaty into question, but could not be held responsible for its breakdown. In this respect Varga thought Mantoux was taking matters a bit too far by holding Keynes responsible for Munich. Mantoux, according to Varga, as a bourgeois economist, simply could not or did not want to understand the existing differences between scientific economics and economics in capitalist countries.

Varga took Mantoux to task for his assertion that there had been no transfer problem in regard to German reparations following Versailles and that this problem had been invented by Keynes. The transfer problem was and is very real indeed, continued Varga, who related the problem to present conditions. He traced the difficulties inherent in this problem for capitalist countries. Socialist countries, he added, do not have unemployment. Hence socialist countries (Poland and Yugoslavia were given as examples) can accept transfers without harming their economies. Reparations after World War II would again be a problem. The USA, England, and France were

57. A. Gusakov, review of F. I. Mikhalevskii, *Zoloto v period mirovykh voin* (Moskva, 1945), *Izvestiya Akademii Nauk SSSR*, Otdelenie Ekonomiki i Prava, 1946, No. 2, p. 174.
58. E. Varga, "Lzheprorok Keins," *Mirovoe Khozyaistvo i Morovaya Politika*, 1947, No. 7, pp. 92–94.

against accepting goods—though France would take coal. "They themselves cannot utilize reparations in the form of industrial goods from current production, but they do not want to grant these goods to the Soviet Union."[59] Mantoux's book was a brave and honest effort, Varga concluded, but very limited on economic analysis.

The examples given above demonstrate the increasing attention devoted to Keynes by the Soviets. Yet this writer failed to find one formal review of *The General Theory*. However, there soon began to appear numerous articles that dealt with Keynes and *The General Theory*. In particular, Professor Blyumin, who appeared to be the most prolific Soviet authority on Western bourgeois economic thought since the war, contributed several articles on this subject within the space of two years.

The first of these was entitled "The London School in Political Economy."[60] Though the article was concerned with the history of this school and its present position on the problems facing the British economy, Blyumin gave considerable attention to Keynes, whose school was placed in opposition to the London school in matters concerning the two main problems in postwar England—crises and unemployment. The emphasis here will be on Blyumin's treatment of Keynes and his school, defined by Blyumin as follows:

One school proceeds from the basis that there are certain organic defects in the very mechanism of capitalistic competition that result in unavoidable disproportions. The latter can be overcome on the basis of a widespread program of state measures based on definite monetary, credit, and industrial policies with the aim of forestalling crises and guaranteeing full employment. Lord Keynes is the most prominent inspirer and ideologist of this school.[61]

The "other school" is what the Soviet writers call "the London school," which they consider to be hostile critics of the Keynesians and the Labour party for their reformist projects to save capitalism. Hayek was especially singled out as a severe critic of Keynes's position.

59. *Ibid.*, p. 94.
60. I. G. Blyumin, "Londonskaya shkola v politicheskoi ekonomii," *Izvestiya Akademii Nauk SSSR*, Otdelenie Ekonomiki i Prava, 1946, No. 3, pp. 217–230.
61. *Ibid.*, p. 218.

On this point the position of Hayek radically differs from Keynes's point of view, since the latter proposed that the basic method of the battle with crises should not consist in holding back production in a "boom" period but, on the contrary, in stimulating industrial expansion and in artificially supporting the general increase of consumer and industrial demand on a high level.[62]

Blyumin found that Keynes had influenced many contemporaries as to the desirability of social works.

The battle between the two schools still continued, Blyumin added, but it was a battle inside the borders of bourgeois economy. Keynes had accepted Marshall on marginal utility as one factor entering into price determination. The goal of both schools was to save capitalism. Keynes was against lowering money wages but did not exclude lowering real wages through inflation. Both schools loathed the socialist revolution and the dictatorship of the proletariat. In fact, their programs were aimed at forestalling the possibility of a revolution and were against "democracy." However, Blyumin held the London school to be the more reactionary of the two.[63]

In the next issue of *Izvestiya*, Blyumin contributed an article entitled "The Economic Teaching of Keynes."[64] This was written shortly after Keynes's death. It was the most complete statement on Keynes found in the literature during the period under review in this chapter. It begins as follows:

Not long ago (April 21, 1946) Lord John Maynard Keynes died. He was one of the most influential economists in contemporary bourgeois literature. His theoretical works have received a great response in the capitalistic countries. All discussions that presently take place among bourgeois economists have, above all, the works of Keynes as their basic axis.[65]

Keynes, Blyumin noted, was distinguished from the majority of professors in that he was not an ivory-tower academic. In this respect he was given due recognition for his services apart from the university community. Blyumin then treated chronologically the major

---

62. *Ibid.*, p. 229.   63. *Ibid.*, p. 230.
64. I. G. Blyumin, "Ekonomicheskoe uchenie Keinsa," *Izvestiya Akademii Nauk SSSR*, Otdelenie Ekonomiki i Prava, 1946, No. 4, pp. 301–319.
65. *Ibid.*, p. 301.

publications of Keynes up to the appearance of *The General Theory*, in order to show the development of his economic thought. Later he discussed *The General Theory* and its influence on bourgeois political economy. He did not mention any further works, as they were not, in his opinion, additions to the theory.

In 1936 Keynes's book *The General Theory of Employment, Interest and Money* was published; in this he presented the most systematic statement of his concepts. The series of ideas which he previously proclaimed in a fragmented manner on the necessity of preventing crises by means of stimulating general demand, on increasing government expenditures, on developing massive social works, received extensive expression in this work. It occupies the central place in the literary works of Keynes. All his later theoretical-economic works are commentaries on this work. It defines the physiognomy of Keynes as an economist. It defines his place in the history of bourgeois economic science.[66]

Blyumin reported that this book had been very well received and had become the center of all theoretical discussions in bourgeois political economy for the past ten years. "It has become the gospel of a new school of bourgeois political economic thought that has written on its banner the battle for the transition to a 'regulated economy,' for the control over the economy that bourgeois economists called 'planned economy.' "[67] Certain economists had described all this as revolutionary, but Blyumin assured his readers that there was nothing revolutionary here at all concerning scientific political economy. Keynes used the methodology of bourgeois political economy. He was a pupil of Marshall and reflected his teaching on cost, capital, and source of profit. What was of interest to the Soviets, according to Blyumin, was that Keynes's views represented the views and the frame of mind of influential bourgeois circles.

Blyumin found that the novelty of Keynes was that he had attempted to create a theory of employment. With this as a starting point, Blyumin reviewed Keynes's main premise of the insufficiency of demand. In Blyumin's analysis, all the Keynesian concepts are presented in a logical order and in an understandable manner. How-

66. *Ibid.*, p. 303.   67. *Ibid.*, p. 303.

ever, Blyumin offered helpful criticisms for the Soviet reader throughout his presentation. In regard to investment increasing employment, he found that Keynes had ignored the fact that in capitalism increasing investment sharpens the contradiction between production and consumption. He charged that Keynes had repeated the error of the underconsumptionists—that is, he had ignored the fact that consumption followed production in conditions of bourgeois society. In Blyumin's opinion the basic defect in Keynes's teaching was that he had shown one single law of demand for all classes. Hence he had overlooked the class nature of consumption in bourgeois society in that the nature of consumption for workers was different from that of capitalists. Blyumin found nothing new in Keynes in regard to underconsumption theory, and, as proof of this, he briefly introduced Hobson and Malthus for support.

Blyumin recognized that investment demand was at the heart of the Keynesian system. He introduced and explained satisfactorily the concepts of the marginal efficiency of capital and the rate of interest. He showed how Keynes, as a vulgar economist, had separated money from investment capital, and as a result, the entrepreneur was viewed as someone separate from the capitalist. And since the rate of profit had to equal or exceed the rate of interest, the latter assumed great importance. "The chief 'novelty' that Keynes brings to interest theory *is in the definition of interest as a pure 'money phenomenon.'* "[68] Blyumin's explanation of this theory presents no difficulty to the reader. His chief criticism of the theory was that it separated interest from capitalist profit. As a result, investment capital was no longer a specific form of capital, and capitalist credit was only a fact of transferring money. Keynes was accused of having incorrectly identified money with investment capital, which explained his assertion that the rate of interest was dependent on the quantity of money. Blyumin felt that Keynes held this concept because it fitted into his scheme to discredit interest and then to regulate it for the benefit of the economy. Blyumin rejected this concept of interest in its entirety.

In regard to the marginal efficiency of capital, Blyumin claimed

68. *Ibid.*, p. 308.

that Keynes had not studied the problem of the source of profit. He found fault with Keynes's psychological explanation of business activity, saying that it skated on the surface of reality and "that it, least of all, is able to explain the basic reasons for economic crises."[69] Also, Keynes had not allotted one word to the effect of monopolies:

He tries to explain the sharpening economic difficulties in the present period by abstracting from the most important peculiarity of capitalism in its highest stage the rule of monopolies. However, it is obvious that the restrictionist policy of monopolists, who are interested in maintaining cartel prices, is one of the most important factors that sharpen economic crisis and delay recovery by braking the flow of new capital investment.[70]

Blyumin found that Keynes had offered no detailed policy as to the method of regulating the economy. This problem was left to his followers, and Beveridge's *Full Employment in a Free Society* was given as an example. Blyumin objected to the confusion of words and terminology in *The General Theory*. Special exception was taken to the use and meaning of such terms as socialism, socialization, and socialization of investment. Despite the misleading confusion over socialism, Blyumin found Keynes's program further strengthening state capitalism.

Blyumin explained the slogan "euthanasia of the rentier" in the following manner. Keynes had thought that the rentier phase of capitalism should be relegated to the past. Many people had thought this revolutionary. Nothing of the sort, Blyumin continued, as this euthanasia applied only to the small rentier, not to financial magnates. Elimination of the small rentier would present no danger for the ruling class of the bourgeoisie. They would have more cheap money available as a result of the disappearance of the small rentier.

Blyumin gave considerable attention to the argument whether a cut in wages could increase employment. He found that Keynes would not reduce money wages but would reduce real wages through inflationary measures. "In this is contained the hidden meaning of the Keynesian theory."[71] The nominalist theory of money was introduced to show that this was part of Keynes's program. Blyumin disagreed with Keynes's contention that inflation would

69. *Ibid.*, p. 312.
70. *Ibid.*, p. 313.   71. *Ibid.*, p. 316.

not result with the wise expansion of money during a period of unemployment. Further, he contended that Keynes had underestimated the dangers of inflation and disregarded its past history.

In his concluding comments, he found Keynes the typical bourgeois ideologist of this period, unable to find the true path to the scientific explanation of crisis because he had identified himself with the self-interests of the bourgeoisie. Blyumin saw that one of Keynes's central ideas was that contemporary capitalism could not develop along old paths of laissez faire and the working of automatic economic forces, and that extraordinary measures had to be taken to save it. According to Blyumin, the bourgeoisie saw in Keynes's doctrine an antidote against the radical plans of socialist democracy and the last bastion against wicked bolshevik planners. "The Keynesian program to save capitalism has a utopian character. It faces a utopian task—to fight crises and unemployment with the preservation of the bases of the capitalistic class."[72] As to the proposals of Keynes with regard to "regulating" capitalism, the effect of these would be negligible; Blyumin quoted Stalin to prove his point. And with this "authoritative" statement he ended his review.

This was the first complete review of *The General Theory*. With allowance made for the Marxian interpolations, Blyumin did a very creditable job in presenting the theory, and his explanations of some of the difficult concepts were exceedingly clear. His criticisms did not interfere with his orderly development of Keynes's thesis, and one would be able to obtain a general idea of the essence of Keynes's thought from it. Especially helpful were the many references to other economists who were either predecessors or followers or even opponents of Keynes. The article contained no equations, diagrams, charts, or statistics. Though this review was long overdue, Blyumin's effort in 1946 probably went a long way to bringing his colleagues up to date.

The following year Keynes was again the subject of an article by Professor Blyumin, "Keynes—the Prophet of 'Regulated Capitalism.' "[73] This article combined to a great extent the two articles discussed earlier, namely, the one on the London school and the one

---

72. *Ibid.*, p. 319.
73. I. G. Blyumin, "Keins—prorok reguliruemogo kapitalizma," *Vestnik Moskovskogo Universiteta*, 1947, No. 4, pp. 43–66.

on the teaching of Keynes. In fact, paragraph after paragraph had been transferred to this article without alteration.

Blyumin conditionally conceded that there was a Keynesian school. This qualification was due first to Keynes himself, who, said Blyumin, had never distinguished himself for the stability of his views, and so there were certain contradictions in his works. Second, it was due to the fact that the most varied social groups had tried to use Keynes's ideas.

Among these different social groups Blyumin included those in prewar Germany. He maintained that Keynesian ideas received a very favorable welcome in the pages of the Hitlerite economic journals *Der Deutsche Volkswirt* and *Die Deutsche Volkswirtschaft*. Blyumin referred to Guillebaud's *The Economic Recovery of Germany* to demonstrate that the ideas of Keynes on full employment had been realized in Germany. Blyumin remembered the defense of Keynes's position on the above question in *The Economist* (London) of April 1, 1936. He also mentioned the correspondence between Keynes and Philip Cortney published in *The Commercial and Financial Chronicle* (August 15, 1946), which discussed the similar views of Keynes and Dr. Schacht. Keynes had promised to explain his views but his sudden death had prevented his doing so. Blyumin added: "It is necessary to note that Keynes himself, though he was not pro-fascist (in the days of Munich he stood out against Neville Chamberlain), did not conceal that his economic theory is 'moderately conservative in its conclusions.' "[74]

At the opposite pole were the reformist circles, particularly among the labor leaders, where Keynesian ideas had received widespread distribution. Blyumin, in answer to his own question why such divergent groups followed after Keynes, gave this explanation. The capitalist world was troubled by the dangers of unemployment and crises. To escape these difficulties, these groups resorted to ideas and measures that when brought together became known as controlled economy, regulated economy, or planned economy. And Blyumin identified Keynes as the main theoretician of these groups that were strengthening state capitalism. Keynes had had an

74. *Ibid.*, p. 44. Here Blyumin cited *The General Theory*, p. 377.

astounding success, and this explained why the bourgeoisie had welcomed him as the new prophet proclaiming the salvation of capitalism.

The article repeated verbatim much of the material found in his previous articles. However, there were several refinements. Among these was the difference between the underconsumptionists and Keynes in regard to saving. The underconsumptionists had accepted that saving would find investment and had seen the danger of too much saving resulting in too much investment. This would create serious disproportions in the economy, thereby disturbing consumption. Keynes, on the other hand, had held that increased saving did not necessarily result either in increased investment or increased consumption.

This article also gave fuller treatment to the secular stagnation thesis concerning the United States. Blyumin warned against misinterpretation in regard to the stagnationists. "It would be incorrect to think that the theory of stagnation gives the conclusion of a fatalistic disposition among bourgeois economists. On the contrary, the supporters of this theory often attempt to emphasize that this theory must play a mobilizing role for all those who are interested in saving capitalism."[75]

Blyumin listed four organic defects in *The General Theory*. First, it had no historical viewpoint. On this point, he cited what he considered to be Keynes's mistaken view of unemployment as an eternal problem and not just as one peculiar to capitalist society. Second, Keynes had wrongly presented the mechanism of capitalist reproduction and concentrated on secondary features. Third, Keynes's analysis had assumed static conditions and unchanging technology. Last, Keynes had refused to consider the harmful effects of monopolies on unemployment.

Blyumin recognized Keynes's influence in the United States and Great Britain and found his influence greater in Britain, where it was being used to bolster the economic base of the Empire. One of the aims of this policy was to weaken the economic dependence on the United States and to isolate the Empire from the harmful

75. *Ibid.*, p. 56.

effects of a crisis in the United States. Blyumin, as a result, found in Keynes three definite class features. "First, he reflects the specific interests of English capitalism; second, he appears as the ideologist of monopoly capital; third, he is the typical bourgeois ideologist in the epoch of the general crisis of capitalism."[76] Blyumin concluded that *The General Theory* would not accomplish its task, and quoted Zhdanov to bring the article to a close.

Though this article was similar to Blyumin's previous ones, it was more hostile toward Keynes. The cold war was beginning to force its proponents into hard and unyielding attitudes. Keynes's ideas were placed in a definite political setting; the Soviet reader was left without any doubts as to the class nature of this doctrine.

Other Soviet economists followed the lead taken by Blyumin. (In view of the increasingly large quantity of criticism on the subject, only the most representative articles and works by the Soviets will receive treatment here.) Professor N. Lyubimov's article "Some Problems of the Economic Theory of Keynes"[77] is an example. Lyubimov's account is of particular interest, as it was he who later translated *The General Theory* into Russian. In this article he followed much the same plan as Blyumin had. Keynes's life and publications were briefly reviewed up to the appearance of *The General Theory*, which is called "the Keynesian Bible" in bourgeois economic literature. Lyubimov's explanations of the Keynesian concepts were none too clear. He took full employment as Keynes's chief aim. He credited Keynes for acknowledging that unemployment was not an accidental guest but a "constant fellow traveler" of the economy. The state was to help achieve full employment by fiscal and monetary policies. The anti-social character of the holders of idle funds was mentioned, and the fact that the state was to combat such people with issues of cheap money. Lyubimov stressed the fact that Keynes had changed the orthodox view with respect to saving, and likewise with interest, which was no longer a reward for delaying consumption but a reward for parting with liquidity.

Lyubimov saw no property equalization measures in Keynes. In

76. *Ibid.*, p. 65.
77. N. Lyubimov, "Nekotorye problemy ekonomicheskoi teorii Keinsa," *Sovetskie Finansy*, 1947, No. 5, pp. 42–48.

regard to monopolies, Keynes had failed to mention that big capital had already penetrated cabinet posts and joined with the bureaucratic leaders. In Lyubimov's analysis, cheap money meant a larger debt, hence more taxes. The workers would have to bear the burden. Such policies would not achieve their aim, for they had been tried before and had failed. The program had no scientific foundation.

Lyubimov recognized that "Keynes appeared in the role of a 'physician' to the sick capitalist system . . . and from the very beginning of his political and literary career to the end of his life was and remained a trusted sword-bearer of the capitalist system."[78] The article ended with Lenin's reference to Keynes's "ugly, savage, and brutal" portrayal of bolshevism. In his refutation of Keynes, Lyubimov made no page references to *The General Theory*.

Academician I. A. Trakhtenberg gave an account of *The General Theory* in his *Capitalist Reproduction and Economic Crises*.[79] His account appeared to be the first treatment of Keynes's work in a general theory text. Trakhtenberg developed the theory of crises chronologically. First he dealt with the predecessors of Marx, namely, Quesnay, Smith, Ricardo, J. S. Mill, Say, and Sismondi. Then special attention was devoted to Marx. Lastly he treated Lenin and Stalin. In the section on Stalin, whose works were held to be the latest contribution to the theory of crises, Trakhtenberg introduced *The General Theory* as the latest representative work of bourgeois political economy that maintained crises were not caused by the capitalist method of production but by accidental circumstances that could be eliminated. "The fullest basis for these views was given by the theory of Keynes, which was developed in *The General Theory* . . . this theory called forth the widest discussion and greatly influenced bourgeois economic thought. At the present time Keynes is the acknowledged leader of bourgeois political economy."[80]

Trakhtenberg noted that Keynes had given insufficient expenditure as a cause for unemployment. Here was a similarity with the

78. *Ibid.*, p. 48.
79. I. A. Trakhtenberg, *Kapitalisticheskoe vosproizvodstvo i ekonomicheskie krizisy* (Leningrad, 1947).
80. *Ibid.*, p. 108.

underconsumptionists but with the essential difference that the old theories "proceeded from the premise that people underconsumed as a consequence of insufficient income, and the apologetic contemporary bourgeois theories proceed from the premise that income is sufficient but that people do not have the propensity to spend it."[81] Trakhtenberg noted that Keynesian proposals on the distribution of income appeared revolutionary at first glance but in reality produced only scanty results.

After explaining the Keynesian concepts, Trakhtenberg dismissed them. "The basic defect of the theory of Keynes and his followers . . . is that they search for the reasons of crises in the sphere of exchange, in the size and character of demand. However, the size and character of demand is caused by production relations."[82]

Many plans had been drawn up recently by different scholars, organizations, and government institutions in the West in order to achieve full employment, and Trakhtenberg maintained that the majority of these were based on Keynesian ideas. "The bourgeois economists obviously prefer the method of Keynes to that of Marx."[83] Trakhtenberg, not unnaturally, opted for Marx and gave due recognition to Stalin for contributions to Marxism. He was reasonably fair toward Keynes, and did not blame him specifically for the promotion of militaristic or imperialist policies. He kept to *The General Theory*, and he provided a very brief but clear summary of its content.

The above works dealing with Keynes frequently commented that *The General Theory* was not really a work of originality. Examples would be given to show the influence on Keynes of the doctrines of his predecessors. This is particularly true of M. V. Kolganov's article "On Mercantilism and Neo-mercantilism in Bourgeois Political Economy."[84] Kolganov maintained that mercantilism was being reevaluated and rehabilitated in works dealing with planned economies, and singled out *The General Theory* for discussion. "Keynes sees the wisdom of the mercantilists in that they consciously stood for lowering the rate of interest by means of holding reserves of

81. *Ibid.*, pp. 109–110.
82. *Ibid.*, p. 112. 83. *Ibid.*, p. 116.
84. M. V. Kolganov, "O merkantilizme i neomerkantilizme v burzhuaznoi politicheskoi ekonomii," *Izvestiya Akademii Nauk SSSR*, Otdelenie Ekonomiki i Prava, 1947, No. 6, pp. 411–428.

money within the country."[85] In Keynes's view, the mercantilists had not accepted the idea of self-regulating interest rates and had even insisted that high interest rates were the chief obstacle to an increase in wealth. Kolganov took issue with Keynes: "In what manner could the rate of interest regulate the movement of capital, production, and employment in the sixteenth and seventeenth centuries when the greater part of the national production was still in feudal forms?"[86] He wondered at all the excitement regarding the novelty of Keynes's theory when Keynes himself had pointed out that the mercantilists were the discoverers of the theory of general employment.

A further article by Professor Blyumin, "The Social-Economic Ideas of Hobson,"[87] dealt with Hobson's rehabilitation by Keynes in *The General Theory*. In Blyumin's evaluation, Keynes had joined Hobson's theory onto *The General Theory* and had even commended Hobson for his scholarly services. The fates had been kinder to Keynes, observed Blyumin, as Hobson's demand for some equalization of income went unnoticed, whereas similar considerations by Keynes had met with stormy success. Blyumin found that the Labour party in England had been influenced by Keynes's view. "This process of the strengthening of the influence of Keynes's ideas in the labor movement as a result of the ideas of Hobson is altogether a characteristic symptom of the general direction of the laborites."[88]

During this period there began to appear articles that took cognizance of Keynes's growing influence on economists and on government policy in the West. For example, "Economic Poverty in the 'Age of Plenty'" by I. Kuzminov[89] was a review of Stuart Chase's *Goals for America*, and dealt with crises and unemployment under capitalism. Chase's book was sharply criticized as a hopeless attempt to explain capitalist reality and justify it. "One of the first attempts of this kind was the book of the famous English economist Keynes, *The General Theory*. . . . Chase's book was undoubtedly written

---

85. *Ibid.*, p. 426.   86. *Ibid.*
87. I. G. Blyumin, "Sotsialno-ekonomicheskie vozzreniya Gobsona," *Izvestiya Akademii Nauk SSSR*, Otdelenie Ekonomiki i Prava, 1947, No. 4, pp. 265–277.
88. *Ibid.*, p. 277.
89. I. Kuzminov, "Ekonomika nishchety v 'vek izobiliya,'" *Bolshevik*, 1946, No. 5, pp. 60–73.

under the influence of Keynes."[90] Kuzminov also reviewed H. Norman Smith's *The Politics of Plenty*,[91] and, recalling Keynes's influence on Chase, he commented: "Now we have to review the reverse situation—the influence of the American Chase on some theoreticians of foggy Albion."[92]

It is interesting to review G. M. Movshovich's article, "The First Postwar Meeting of the American Economists,"[93] which is an account of the papers and proceedings of the fifty-eighth annual meeting of the American Economic Association. Movshovich reported that the overwhelming majority of economists identified the economic difficulties following World War II, but failed to get at the heart of the matter. "In their attempts to find common ground for measures of 'salvation,' their views at first turn naturally to Keynes."[94] Movshovich found that Keynes was compared to Adam Smith. There was some truth in this, for Keynes had captured the bourgeoisie of his day just as Smith had, the difference being that capitalism was now in a general state of crisis. In dealing with full-employment projects, Movshovich noted: "With the theoretical conceptions of Keynes are tightly bound the attempts to remove the greatest sore of contemporary capitalism—massive unemployment —by means of these or those measures existing in the framework of the present economic system."[95]

M. Smit, a woman economist, discussed *The General Theory* and its influence in an article "In Search of Capitalism without Crisis."[96] Commenting on some of the plans and projects appearing at the end of the war, she noted that unemployment remained the biggest problem. She quoted Amlie to the effect that the problem could be solved either through Marx or through Keynes.[97] She then discussed the

90. *Ibid.*, p. 64.
91. I. Kuzminov, "Ekonomika nishchety i 'politika izobilya,'" *Bolshevik*, 1946, Nos. 7–8, pp. 76–88.
92. *Ibid.*, p. 76.
93. G. M. Movshovich, "Pervyi poslevoennyi sezd amerikanskikh ekonomistov," *Izvestiya Akademii Nauk SSSR*, Otdelenie Ekonomiki i Prava, 1947, No. 3, pp. 190–200.
94. *Ibid.*, p. 192.   95. *Ibid.*, p. 193.
96. M. Smit, "V poiskakh bezkrizisnogo kapitalizma," *Planovoe Khozyaistvo*, 1946, No. 6, pp. 75–89.
97. *Ibid.*, p. 76. Though Smit gave no particulars for her reference to Amlie, she was presumably referring to Thomas R. Amlie, "Full Employment After the War," *The Nation*, Supplement, Nov. 27, 1943, pp. 625–652.

notorious "revolution" due to *The General Theory*. "At first the book did not evoke much interest, but in the war years it became in its way the gospel of 'transformed' capitalism. . . . Beveridge in his . . . *Full Employment in a Free Society* (1945) speaks of a 'new era' that entered with the publication of *The General Theory* of Keynes."[98] Smit examined Keynes's theory and found that Keynes had remained silent on a number of questions and that perhaps his success was due to this silence.[99] Smit's decidedly limited knowledge of Western economists is apparent from the reference in her article to "Seymour and Harris as joint authors, together with Hansen, of a series of articles in *The New Republic*."[100]

I. Lemin's survey, "Ideology and Policy of Laborism in the Service of Imperialist Reaction,"[101] found that English right-wing labor leaders had taken their places in the reactionary ranks in the international struggle between the imperialist and democratic camps. Lemin found that they were opportunists who deceived the workers. In economic policy they followed Keynes: "The English Labour party has made the Keynesian theory its economic credo. Right-wing laborites call themselves pupils of Keynes and refer to him as an unquestionable authority. With special zealousness they repeat the assertions of Keynes about the possibility of a planned economy under capitalism."[102]

From the foregoing it is clear that the Soviet writers readily acknowledged the influence of Keynes on Britain. Toward the end of the period under review in this chapter, the emphasis shifts to the influence of Keynes in the United States. With this development, increasing attention is given to connecting Keynes with American policy. A. Aizenshadt's article "The Learned Servants of American Capital"[103] is an early example.

Aizenshadt found capitalism to be in great difficulties in America, and he reviewed works by Higgins, Henderson, Hansen, Harris, and others in support of his viewpoint. The American Economic As-

98. *Planovoe Khozyaistvo*, 1946, No. 6, p. 76.
99. *Ibid.*, p. 80.   100. *Ibid.*, p. 84.
101. I. Lemin, "Ideologiya i politika leiborizma na sluzhbe imperialisticheskoi reaktsii," *Bolshevik*, 1948, No. 6, pp. 43–62.
102. *Ibid.*, p. 47.
103. A. Aizenshadt, "Uchenye prisluzhniki amerikanskogo kapitala," *Planovoe Khozyaistvo*, 1947, No. 4, pp. 80–89.

sociation's *Readings in Business Cycle Theory* was one of the works reviewed as representative of the efforts to come to terms with the crisis of capitalism. In Aizenshadt's opinion, all the contributors to the above volume were Keynesians, and Alvin Hansen was the acknowledged head of the Keynesians in America. *The General Theory* had provided a new way to exploit the worker, who had to reduce his propensity to consume to provide funds for investment.[104] Bourgeois economists, however, did not stop at internal policies to solve crises but counted on monopoly capital and imperialism. The "notorious" Truman Doctrine and Marshall Plan as well as the theories of the American economists were evidence of the development of imperialist expansion.[105]

L. Alter wrote on the same theme in his "The Theoretical Swordbearers of American Imperialism,"[106] which reviewed the past trends in American economic thought as well as the present position of bourgeois economic thought. American economists were found to support imperialism and a reduction in the living standard of the workers. Alter held that the Keynesian theory was widely used for the latter purpose, and referred to the political orientation of this theory in citing the preface to the German edition of *The General Theory*, in which Keynes had written that his theory could be more easily adapted to the conditions of a totalitarian state.[107]

Professor Blyumin summed up the Soviet position on this theme with his "American Economists in the Service of Monopolies,"[108] written just prior to the publication of the Russian translation of *The General Theory*. In short, Blyumin found that the United States could not use its industrial capacity to the full, and many economists (Ayres, Lorwin, Hansen) had made proposals to solve this dilemma. "The inspirer of these numerous, but at the same time unfruitful projects of 'healing' capitalism was the English economist Keynes, the fashionable prophet of 'regulated capitalism' and the typical bourgeois ideologist of the epoch of the general crisis of

---

104. *Ibid.*, p. 82.   105. *Ibid.*, p. 85.
106. L. Alter, "Teoreticheskie oruzhenostsy americanskogo imperializma," Obzor Literatury, *Planovoe Khozyaistvo*, 1947, No. 5, pp. 74–94.
107. *Ibid.*, p. 87.
108. I. G. Blyumin, "Amerikanskie ekonomisty na sluzhbe monopolii," *Voprosy Ekonomiki*, 1948, No. 8, pp. 52–65.

capitalism."[109] Also: "The ideas of anti-crisis policy, which Keynes created, play in our time an altogether significant role in determining the economic policy of the American government."[110]

Blyumin attributed the aggressiveness of the American followers of Keynes to an article by Keynes[111] which had observed that the success or failure of the employment policies of capitalist democracy in the United States could not be evaluated because of the intervention of the war. In Blyumin's opinion, Keynes's American followers had actually used the war to increase demand and solve the problem of unemployment: "This idea was well mastered by the American followers of Keynes. The use of war and military preparation as 'safety valves' for crises is one of the basic, although often hidden, motives for the war psychology fanned by the reactionary American press at the present."[112] This safety valve, Blyumin concluded, might increase demand but it would also bring capitalism closer to destruction.

The analysis of the foregoing articles and works by Soviet economists from the date of the English publication of *The General Theory* up to 1948, when the first Russian translation appeared, shows that the Soviets were slow to recognize the significance of Keynes's major work. However, once their Western colleagues had made it the focal point of their economic discussions, the Soviets could no longer afford to ignore its impact on the development of economic thought in the capitalist countries. The increasing attention given by the Soviets to Keynes and in particular to his *General Theory* resulted in a spate of articles and writings that were devoted wholly or in part to an examination of Keynes and his influence. At first the Soviets referred to Keynes on a level with other economists such as Cassel, Wicksell, and Mitchell. Then they gave the followers of Keynes's ideas the status of an economic school, and it was examined and contrasted with other schools, such as the London and the Harvard schools. Finally, the Keynesian school, in the Soviet view, triumphed, and became the predominant school in bourgeois political economy.

109. *Ibid.*, p. 56.   110. *Ibid.*, p. 62.
111. J. M. Keynes, "The United States and the Keynes Plan," *The New Republic*, July 29, 1940, pp. 156–159.
112. Blyumin, *Voprosy Ekonomiki*, 1948, No. 8, p. 65.

The tardiness of Soviet economists in recognizing *The General Theory* can be explained by a number of factors. *The General Theory* was not an immediate success in the West. During the pre-war period the Soviets were very busy with their internal problems, which included industrial planning and political purges—the latter having a decided effect on intellectual objectivity and effort. Then came the war with its attendant dislocations, and all efforts were concentrated on national defense. Finally, with the war's end, the Soviets had time to take stock of current Western economic developments and found that Keynesian ideas had become dominant. Blyumin even noticed and quoted the famous remark: "We are all Keynesians now."[113] As a result of the influence of Keynesian ideas on the economic policies in Great Britain and the United States, the Soviets could no longer ignore *The General Theory* and were forced to consider its implications.

The advent of the cold war brought *The General Theory* into sharper focus for the Soviets. They saw the ideas of Keynes as providing a basis for imperialist aggression. Keynes, the bourgeois economist, had now become an ideologist of monopoly capitalism. As a result, *The General Theory* was even more important for the Soviet appraisal of the Western position. At this time, the decision was probably taken to have *The General Theory* translated into Russian.

113. Blyumin, *Vestnik Moskovskogo Universiteta*, 1947, No. 4, p. 45.

IV. *The Russian translation of* The General Theory of Employment, Interest and Money

Since *The General Theory* first appeared in English in 1936, it has gone through several reprintings and has been translated into the major languages of the world. It was translated into the Russian language in 1948; the translation was reprinted in 1949.

One might think that the best translation of a work would be an exact replica of the original. However, there are difficulties in producing a literal translation since meaning, interpretation, syntax, rhythm, and style vary from language to language and from translator to translator. If, in addition, the translator has a strong viewpoint on the subject matter, then the translation may differ to a significant degree from the original. A case in point is made by Anna Balakian, a literary critic, concerning the French translation by Clemence Royer of *The Origin of Species*. Darwin described Royer as a deist and hater of Christianity who believed that natural selection would explain everything. In fact, Royer added footnotes to the translation to explain even the author's doubts away. Hence, according to Anna Balakian, the French received an unusually strong and positive version of *The Origin of Species*.[1] Bearing this example in mind, the present writer thought it necessary to examine the Russian translation of *The General Theory* in order to appraise the accuracy of the version available to the Soviet public.

The translation of 1948[2] is the only one in the Soviet literature and is assumed to have been authorized by the authorities. However, since the Soviets are not a party to the international copyright

---

1. Anna Balakian, *Surrealism* (New York, 1959), p. 25.
2. Although references to the Russian edition of *The General Theory* were plentiful, to obtain a copy of this work proved impossible. A thorough search of the major Slavic holdings in the United States failed to produce one. As a result, microfilm copies of the 1948 and 1949 editions, obtained as a result of a research trip to the Soviet Union in 1963, served as the basis for this assessment of the Russian translation.

convention, this translation was not officially authorized by the legal representatives of the author. The official Russian translator was Professor N. N. Lyubimov, the editor was G. Movshovich, the technical editor was A. Nikiferova, and the proofreaders were N. Bulgakov and O. Shmelev. The translation was completed and received at the typesetter's on July 7, 1948. It went to press on November 29, 1948. This edition carried a forty-five page introductory article by Professor Blyumin, whose name appeared on the title page together with Lyubimov's.[3] The second printing appeared in 1949, and only Professor Lyubimov was listed on the title page. Professor Blyumin's name was omitted and his article was not included. Otherwise the two printings were identical in every respect. The first impression, which carried Blyumin's article, will be the version considered in this chapter. Although the translation did not appear until twelve years after the original, it is significant that it appeared as early as it did in the postwar period. At this time there were few translations of foreign economic works and the majority of these were generally unfavorable accounts of Western economic society, portraying wealth inequality or the size of monopolies. In this respect, it was a tribute to Keynes's international standing to have his work translated into Russian.

In his lengthy introduction, Blyumin noted that one of the manifestations of the general crisis of capitalism was the general crisis in bourgeois ideology, particularly in bourgeois political economy. This was even more apparent with the division of the world into the capitalist and the socialist systems:

> The victory of socialism in our country dealt a powerful blow to bourgeois political economy, whose vital mission was based on the "establishment" of the immortality and indestructability of capitalism. The results of the socialist construction in the USSR utterly crushed the attempts of countless legions of bourgeois apologists to "prove" the impossibility of a socialist economy.[4]

3. Soviet authors use forewords and prefaces, words which have Russian equivalents. The significance of an "introductory" article in this case was to provide a suitable interpretation of the work before the reader embarked on the body of the text.

4. Dzh. M. Keins, *Obshchaya teoriya zanyatosti, protsenta i deneg* (Moskva, 1948), p. v. Hereinafter cited as Keins, *Teoriya*.

As a result of these new historical developments, bourgeois political economy had undergone certain changes. However, Blyumin noted that the apology for capitalism was still the basic content of vulgar economics. This apology, Blyumin explained, took various forms in different historical periods. Now the bourgeois economists faced new tasks:

The bourgeois apologists are presently occupied in strengthening the tottering edifice of capitalism. Extolling the pure automatic working of the laws of competition cannot satisfy the bourgeoisie any more. As a result of the large-scale economic convulsions, all kinds of projects of "perfecting," "reorganizing," and "healing" capitalism have received great popularity.[5]

At present the bourgeois economists dared not risk an open defense of capitalism as the perfect system. Instead they were trying to convince the masses that the shortcomings of capitalism could be put right without touching the rule of monopoly.

This change of method, according to Blyumin, reflected the growth of the contradictions of capitalism. It had the direct purpose of defrauding the masses and was dependent on factors such as the role of state intervention in the bourgeois economy as well as on the existing laws of capitalism.

The bourgeois apologists attempt to inculcate the faith in the masses that the bourgeois state with its intervention can correct the shortcomings of the capitalist mechanism. Modern bourgeois political economy has virtually rejected objective economic laws and has substituted for them faith in an all-powerful bourgeois state.
The crisis of bourgeois political economy is reflected most distinctly in Keynesianism.[6]

Having thus situated Keynesianism in the context of a barrage of criticism directed at bourgeois political economy, Blyumin went on to quote from William Z. Foster, the American Communist, to the effect that Keynes was the physician to capitalism and the world's leading bourgeois economist. Blyumin continued with his introduction of Keynes. Three features, Blyumin cautioned his readers, should be kept in mind in order to understand Keynesianism cor-

5. *Ibid.*, p. vii.   6. *Ibid.*, pp. viii–ix.

rectly: first, Keynes's own lengthy critique of the shortcomings of capitalism; second, his deliberate opposition to the supporters of the old vulgar bourgeois economics; and third, his introduction of radical slogans to deceive the masses. Blyumin found that Keynes thus outwardly appeared to be a radical. He recalled Keynes's fight against unemployment, his opposition to cutting money wages, his mention of property inequality, and his anti-war position. But in reality, Blyumin maintained with determination, Keynes's program was clearly reactionary. "The basic aim of Keynes is to strengthen the position of monopoly capital at the expense of the working class with the help of the use of state measures."[7]

Blyumin gave the following examples to demonstrate the reactionary character of Keynes's program. His fight against unemployment was not an honest effort but a tricky maneuver, for it involved reducing real wages. The state regulation of capital investment was a smoke screen to fatten capitalists' profits. Blyumin recalled the sale of industrial plants built by the US government during the war. These were built by taxpayer's money and then given to monopoly capitalists. The state assumed the expense and the risk but the capitalists received the profits, which were strongly guaranteed. Such was the real essence of the Keynesian program, though this meaning was deeply and carefully hidden in his theory.

Blyumin saw Keynes as the ideologist of monopoly capital generally, but first and foremost as the ideologist of British imperialism. According to Blyumin, this was not accidental, because decaying capitalism first appeared in England and hence she was ready for all sorts of projects to cure capitalism. Although Keynesianism originated in England, Blyumin found that it had received international attention. Also, since Keynes had not spelled out in any detail his political program, it had been adopted by various reactionary groups having state capitalistic tendencies regardless of their differing political views. At this point, Schacht, Hitler and Truman were quoted as sympathetic or having been sympathetic to Keynes's ideas.

Blyumin, however, gave particular attention to the right-wing socialists throughout the world who accepted the Keynesian program. Through the right-wing socialists, Keynesian ideas penetrate the work-

7. *Ibid.,* p. x.

ing class. Keynesianism sows among the workers the harmful illusion of the possibility of overcoming crises and unemployment within the framework of capitalist society. The fight against Keynesianism is one of the most important tasks of the ideological work of Marxist economic science.[8]

And in this fight, Blyumin concluded, the Russian translation of Keynes's basic work would present the opportunity for a wider circle of Soviet economists to join in the criticism of Keynesianism.

The above ended the first section of Blyumin's introductory article. He felt sure that a detailed criticism of Keynes's theory would be forthcoming from Soviet economists on the basis of the translation available to them. He then proceeded to give a summary criticism of the basic tenets of Keynes's theory and to uncover its social-political thought. Blyumin had dealt with the majority of these criticisms in his earlier works. This chapter will mention only his major objections and give attention to any new viewpoint on his part.

Blyumin repeated his objections to Keynes's claim to be a heretic. To prove his assertion, he again reviewed Keynes's debt to Marshall. He also objected to Keynes's list of economists belonging to the classical school. This school, he contended, ended with J. S. Mill. Keynes, it was found, had accepted the postulates of the Cambridge school, excepting the one concerning unemployment. "In the person of Keynes, bourgeois economic theory acknowledged, finally, the elementary fact that there exists involuntary unemployment that does not depend at all on the marginal disutility of labor."[9]

He gave Keynes credit for recognizing the existence of the problem of unemployment, but criticized him for his views on wage policy. Blyumin found Keynes's position that real and money wages move in the opposite directions absurd. Keynes himself had to admit that this question needed additional research, and Blyumin

8. *Ibid.*, p. xiv. The last two sentences were quoted by Professor Yohe of Duke University in a letter in defense of Keynes to *The New York Times*, July 30, 1961, p. 10E. Yohe subsequently received an inquiry from A. M. Schlesinger, Jr., then a special assistant to President Kennedy, requesting the full reference. Yohe replied that he had found this quotation in a Swedish source—an article by Lief Bjork, "En Sovjetekonom om Stockholmsskolan [A Soviet Economist on the Stockholm School]," *Ekonomisk Tidskrift*, LXII (Dec., 1960), 233–249.

9. Keins, *Teoriya*, p. xvi.

quoted him on this position.[10] Blyumin found that Keynes had proceeded from the metaphysical theory of equilibrium and had made some adjustments to it. Previously, equilibrium meant full utilization of all resources including labor, but Keynes had recognized that unemployment could exist with the economy in equilibrium.

Blyumin then gave a ten-point summary of *The General Theory* that dealt with Keynes's main propositions.[11] He found that Keynes's methodology was unscientific as it was penetrated to the full with "idealism and metaphysics." Also, Keynes's theory was non-historical. As a result Keynes was able to avoid the true problem of unemployment as related to the capitalist method of production. Blyumin also held that Keynes's explanation of the psychological factors affecting economic forces was based on his superficial "idealistic" method. The propensity to consume was especially singled out as being unhistorical and idealistic. Keynes had seen every society as a whole suffering from insufficient demand. Since, according to Blyumin, Keynes had one law for all of society, he had thus been able to avoid the problem of the relative and absolute impoverishment of the worker. Blyumin maintained that the propensity to consume and the propensity to save applied only to capitalists, but that Keynes had been silent on this point.

Blyumin recognized the decisive role that investment played in Keynes's theory. According to him, Keynes had made only one connection between investment and consumption. This was that investment would increase employment, income, and consumption through the effect of the multiplier. Blyumin thought Keynes and his followers had overestimated the value of the multiplier, and that Keynes had overlooked the fact that increased investment would increase production but not necessarily consumption because of the restricted consumption base in capitalist society. Further, Blyumin contended that even if consumption increased, it could be handled by existing idle capacity without resorting to increased investment.

In dealing with investment, Blyumin found that Keynes had

10. *Ibid.*, p. xvii. Blyumin gave the following reference: Keynes, "Relative Movements of Real Wages and Output," *Economic Journal* (March, 1939), p. 34.
11. Keins, *Teoriya*, pp. xviii–xx.

avoided the real issues by resorting to the device known as the propensity to invest. Here the rate of interest played a significant role as it limited the amount of investment. Blyumin maintained that the above scheme was based on three incorrect assumptions: first, the use of loan capital alone by the entrepreneur; second, the "notorious" law of diminishing returns; and third, the belief that monopolies could be ignored.[12] Keynes had reassessed the role of the rate of interest. Accumulation of capital had been a source of difficulty to Keynes, but he had admitted that under modern conditions the marginal efficiency of capital could be driven to zero. This development was supposed to bring about social changes and remove some of the repulsive features from capitalism. Blyumin found this a source of amusement: "What a cheerful picture Keynes paints. This is a new version of the theory of the automatic self-liquidation of capitalist profit as the result of the fantastic surplus of capital."[13]

Blyumin sharply criticized the role Keynes had assigned to psychological factors in determining the profitability of capital or the marginal efficiency of capital. Changes from optimism to pessimism in the mood of the investor explained nothing. Likewise with the rate of interest, Blyumin found that the stock exchange and speculation played too important a role in Keynes's theory. Keynes had separated the rate of interest from profit. Keynes's analysis of the demand for money was found to be too abstract and not historical enough. Keynes, contended Blyumin, had no real explanation of the rate of interest. Liquidity preference was too psychological an interpretation to be acceptable. Further, the quantity of credit was independent of the quantity of money. Keynes had tried to discredit high interest rates. Then he had wanted to regulate interest rates to benefit the capitalists.

After a review of Chapter XVIII of *The General Theory*, Blyumin maintained that this chapter in particular demonstrated Keynes's defective, anti-scientific methodology. He listed the following five short-comings. First, Keynes's method was too static, for it assumed too many constants. Second, the theory was too subjec-

12. *Ibid.*, p. xxvii.   13. *Ibid.*, p. xxviii.

tive, for it depended to a significant degree on the three psychological factors. Third, the theory did not mention capitalist monopolies and finance capital. Fourth, the theory avoided the basic class contradiction of capitalism resulting from the category of surplus value. Fifth, the theory accepted the vulgar quantity of money theory in its analysis.[14] This last defect gave theoretical support to inflationary policies. Keynes, according to Blyumin, had rehabilitated inflationary methods and had advocated expansion of the money supply to stimulate investment. Blyumin thought this to be a very dangerous course.

In the third and final section of his introduction, Blyumin presented additional criticisms and then gave his conclusions on *The General Theory*. The theory, Blyumin contended, was an open apology for monopoly capital, but it contained plenty of social demagoguery. Keynes had attacked only the minor defects of the system. He had not assaulted the commanding heights of finance capital. Further, Blyumin found that Keynes had not even considered unemployment to be a law of capitalism. Keynes considered unemployment just a defect of capitalism. There were no special measures existing to deal with it until his theory appeared. This, according to Blyumin, was the main conclusion of Keynes's theory —to "heal," to "restore," and to "reorganize" capitalism.

Keynes's way to strengthen capitalism, in Blyumin's view, was simply to strengthen monopoly capitalism. Blyumin found that this was to be done by the state control of investment, but Keynes would not touch the "holy of holies," that is, private capitalist property. Keynes had wanted to save capitalism, even though conservatives might misinterpret him. Blyumin did not think this misinterpretation possible.[15] In Blyumin's view, the imperialist state was to serve as an executive committee for monopoly affairs. The taxpayers would pay for the investment, which would, in turn, be handed over to the monopolists. This method, Blyumin noted, was a legitimate way of stealing from the treasury. This was the sort of regulation or planning that, in Blyumin's opinion, Keynes had in mind. Blyu-

14. *Ibid.*, p. xxxiv.
15. However, this has in fact been the case. See my remarks on the Veritas Foundation's assessment of Keynes in chap. viii.

min stoutly maintained that scientific planning occurred only in the USSR.

He found that the workers always suffered under Keynes's scheme. The real bourgeois essence of Keynes was revealed in his wage program. "It is not accidental that Keynes viewed the 'wage unit' as one of the independent variables that defined the level of employment."[16] Blyumin asserted that rising wages would threaten full employment in the Keynesian scheme, hence wages were to be regulated in the interests of the capitalists. Blyumin maintained that Keynes had a definite bias against the workers. He recalled that Keynes had pointed out that the mercantilists kept wages low and that the capitalists of the nineteenth century also knew how to keep wages down. By implication Blyumin charged Keynes with favoring weak trade unions in order to facilitate employment. The Keynesian method of attacking wages through inflationary measures, which would reduce real wages revealed, according to Blyumin, the consistency of Keynes's attitude toward the workers.

Blyumin noted that the bourgeois economists proposed two methods to reduce wages. One was through a reduction of money wages, and the other was through a reduction of real wages by means of an inflationary policy. In the first method, the private entrepreneur reduced money wages and there was no need of governmental interference. The second method, which Keynes had advocated, involved interference by the state. This was the essential difference that Blyumin saw in comparing these plans.[17] So the method of reducing real wages was inseparably bound to state-monopoly capitalism.

As a result of Keynes's teaching on the regulation of the economy, Blyumin held, state-monopoly capitalism had become tightly connected with the growth of militarism. The Keynesian concepts, Blyumin noted, were especially suited to be a basis for a program of militarization. Blyumin added that Keynes had not explored the reasons for war but had mentioned its beneficial influence on general demand. Here again Blyumin recalled that Keynes had seen how wars had increased the efficiency of capital in the nineteenth century. Keynes's followers had seized on his theory that war increased

16. Keins, *Teoriya*, p. xl.   17. *Ibid.*, p. xlii.

demand, and hoped thereby to correct capitalism's fatal defect. Keynes presented himself as an objective scholar, but Blyumin noted that his theory served imperialism:

In his *General Theory of Employment* Keynes forged an ideological weapon for the justification of imperialist expansion. In this is reflected the reactionary essence of his theory. Although Keynes in his book refrained from an open formulation of imperialist conclusions, such conclusions can easily be drawn from his theory.[18]

Blyumin even introduced *How to Pay for the War* to show what he considered to be Keynes's rooted class prejudice in favor of the bourgeoisie. He reminded his readers to bear three definite class features of Keynes in mind. First, his theory reflected the interests of a definite circle of monopoly capitalists. Second, he reflected the specific interests of the powerful English bourgeoisie. Third, his theory reflected the typical characteristics of bourgeois ideology in the general crises of capitalism.[19] All the features of his system, especially recognition of unemployment and liquidity preference, demonstrated the instability of capitalism.

The projects of Keynes and his followers to rejuvenate capitalism were called reactionary. The American economists were singled out as basing their expansionist theories on Keynes. Blyumin refused to consider Keynes in any way equal to Adam Smith. Nevertheless, he admitted that Keynes was the new prophet called in to save capitalism. His message, as interpreted by Blyumin, was that only small adjustments were necessary for this purpose. These small changes would enable capitalism to avoid the great changes associated with a revolutionary uprising. Blyumin attributed the enthusiastic reception of Keynes's theory to the hopes that the bourgeoisie placed in it as a defense against the growing influence of the ideas of Marxism-Leninism.

Blyumin had conclusive evidence that Keynes was a foe of Marxism and quoted the passage from *Essays in Persuasion* in which Keynes expresses little faith in the proletariat and describes the bourgeoisie and the intelligentsia as the salt of the earth and the bearers of progress. Blyumin objected to Keynes's referring to Marxism as

18. *Ibid.*, p. xliv.   19. *Ibid.*, p. xlvi.

a religion, and placing Marx on a level with Silvio Gesell: "In *The General Theory of Employment, Interest and Money* Keynes demonstratively places Gesell, a mediocre bourgeois economist who published a charlatan project for stabilizing money circulation, in the same rank as Marx."[20] He found that even such an "arrant" bourgeois economist as Schumpeter objected to this ordering.

Blyumin called for a categorical rebuff to those false attempts to bring together the reactionary theory of Keynes with the "immortal" theory of the great Marx. These fashionable attempts to weave Marxism into the theory of Keynes he regarded as reformist tricks to distort Marxism. "In reality the basic meaning of Keynesianism is to undermine the influence of Marxism-Leninism and place in opposition to it this hostile ideology permeated with a spirit of an apology for monopolistic capital."[21] Previous attempts in the form of the Austrian school, Fabianism, and Sombartism had failed to overthrow Marx, and Blyumin concluded his lengthy introductory article by predicting this same fate for Keynesianism.

Blyumin's lengthy introduction revealed the dangers of Keynesianism clearly to his Soviet readers. It was followed by a short note from Lyubimov, the translator, which discussed the difficulties in translating Keynes's book. Lyubimov said that the book was full of complicated and involved abstractions and quasi-mathematical equations. It was necessary to know the exact meaning of the terms to follow Keynes's presentation. Since Keynes used terms that were not applicable to Soviet economic literature when translated into Russian, Lyubimov found it necessary to introduce these new terms and define them. They were as follows: frictional unemployment, factor costs, disutility of labor, multiplier, and disinvestment. Lyubimov's definitions were adequate and helpful.

Keynes's preface to *The General Theory* was omitted in the Russian translation. In his preface Keynes addressed his book chiefly to his fellow economists and made a brief statement as to its purpose. Not only was the preface omitted in its entirety, but there was no statement in the translation regarding its existence.

The translation, apart from certain omissions, was a faithful ren-

---

20. *Ibid.*, p. xlviii.   21. *Ibid.*, p. xlix.

dering of the original. The only change in the format of the work was that the index was split into two sections, one for the names of individuals and the other for the subject matter proper. Lyubimov's translation presented a scholarly and highly readable account of the work. Considering the difficulty of the task, his effort must be termed excellent.

The editor, G. Movshovich, made numerous comments in the form of footnotes, always identified as his own. Some were merely of help to a Soviet reader; others, of a more subjective nature, were of considerable interest because they revealed a strong political bias against Keynes's work. The editor must also be held responsible for certain important omissions in the text. In these respects, the translation was presented in a different light from the original. A summary of the editorial comments and a note of his omissions will serve to evaluate his contribution.

On page 21 of *The General Theory* Keynes discussed the assumption of equality of the demand price and supply price. In the translation, this passage was footnoted and this editorial comment was given:

Keynes mechanically and uncritically borrowed the terms "supply price" and "demand price" as well as the theory of prices from Marshall. [Here followed the appropriate quotation from Marshall's *Principles of Economics*, p. 142.] In the quality of one of the greatest, most orthodox representatives of vulgar bourgeois eclectics, Marshall completely refused to analyze the substance of cost and attempted to explain prices by the interaction among demand, supply, and the costs of production, although Marx irrefutably proved that such "explanations" by their essence present their own vicious circle because the costs of production, demand, and supply themselves are dependent on prices. In these conditions, Keynes's explanations of the level and movement of prices are limited to repetition of the vulgar chatter of Marshall. This sufficiently characterizes the "scientific" level of the "cunning" constructions that were developed on this basis in the following chapters.[22]

In discussing effective demand on page 32 of *The General Theory*, Keynes mentioned "the underworlds of Karl Marx, Silvio Gesell or Major Douglas." This remark inevitably drew blood:

In his blind hatred of Marx and Marxism, Keynes attempts to

22. *Ibid.*, pp. 21–22.

place the genius who founded scientific socialism in the same ranks of third-rate petty bourgeois utopians and calls Marxism the "underworld" of political economy. In reality, Marx alone was able to give an explanation of the insufficiency of demand in capitalist society. Marx showed that the shortage of demand (i.e., in other words, overproduction) inevitably flows from the class structure of capitalist society, from the contradictions between the social character of production and the private capitalist form of appropriation, and from the absolute and relative impoverishment of the working class. It is also known that V. I. Lenin brilliantly developed further the theory of the capitalist markets. In comparison with these original scientific discoveries, the obscure references of Keynes to the changes in the psychology of society (which he is in no position to explain) produce, in truth, a pathetic impression.[23]

On page 63 of *The General Theory*, Keynes, in formulating his savings=investment identity, maintained that it was in keeping with common sense and with the traditional usage of the great majority of economists. After the word "economists," the editor's footnote explained: "Here, as in other places in the book, under the word 'economists' the author means the representatives of bourgeois economic thought."[24]

On page 67 of his "Appendix on User Cost," Keynes stated that the supply price in the short run equaled marginal factor cost. The editor challenged this sentence with this footnote:

It is superfluous to say that so-called "newest theory" in its essence repeats all the old mistakes and errors. The impossibility of determining value from the cost of production was exhaustively and fully proved by Marx. The attempts of recent bourgeois theoreticians to connect value not with average, but with "marginal" costs of production, you understand, do not save the situation. This way or that way all constructions revolve in a vicious circle because "marginal costs" can be determined only from existing prices, which in turn have to be explained by the costs of production. The thinking on marginal costs of production attempts to smooth over the question of the source of capitalist profits. These bourgeois theoreticians whom Keynes has in mind attempt to connect the price only with several elements of the costs of production and merely confuse the question still further.[25]

On page 104 of *The General Theory*, Keynes made the following

23. *Ibid.*, p. 31.
24. *Ibid.*, p. 61.   25. *Ibid.*, p. 64.

statement: "Consumption—to repeat the obvious—is the sole end of all economic activity." The editor had this to remark: "This abstract, non-historical formulation of the question obviously has nothing to do with reality. It is known that in the conditions of capitalism the aim of economic activity is not consumption at all, but the extraction of surplus profits."[26]

On page 106 of *The General Theory*, Keynes discussed the public's concern that public investment would create future difficulties. The editor made these observations:

Here Keynes portrays the matter as though the subject were the absolute satiation of demand, as if dwelling houses, factories, and plants could be constructed in the conditions of capitalism in such quantities that they would, in reality, be in surplus. But the fact is that "satiated demand" only occurs because the working masses as the result of a systematic lowering of their living standards and the limiting of their income are in no condition to buy the products that they badly need and by necessity they suffer cruel want.[27]

On page 163 Keynes mentioned a class of investments undertaken by public authority that were influenced by the expectancy of social advantages. The editor disagreed as to these influences:

Here again Keynes crudely distorts and whitewashes capitalist reality. The assertion that the government and municipal authorities in their investments "are proceeding on the premises of the prospective social advantages" is false through and through. In reality these authorities find themselves in their entirety under the control of capitalist monopolies and act in their interests. These authorities carry out investment only when the capitalists need some sort of construction on which they do not want to spend their own money or when it is necessary to procure profitable orders or to guarantee for themselves the possibility of offering inactive capital funds to receive interest that is paid by the taxpayers, etc., etc.[28]

On page 194 Keynes introduced the income velocity of money in connection with the demand for money. The editor gave his interpretation of income velocity to the reader:

26. *Ibid.*, p. 99. Alongside the editor's comment someone had written "blockhead" in the 1949 edition.
27. *Ibid.*, p. 101.   28. *Ibid.*, pp. 155–156.

Income velocity of money is a term that was introduced by a number of English bourgeois economists in their attempts to save the quantity theory of money, which was completely lost in contradictions. These economists propose to review the total supply of money in connection with the total sum of income of the population. The "income velocity of money" is thus defined as the division of the general total of income by the quantity of money. It is understood that all this is purely formalistic exercise and does not at all provide an explanation of the actual lawful development of the capitalist economy since bourgeois political economy is in no state to explain the quantity of income or the different classes of society or the quantity of money appearing in exchange.[29]

In dealing with wage policy on page 267 Keynes said: "Except in a socialized community where wage-policy is settled by decree, there is no means of securing uniform wage reductions for every class of labour." The editor took issue with Keynes:

This assertion represents a slander on socialist society prompted by the hatred and fear that socialism inspires in Keynes. He does not understand, and he does not want to understand, the laws of socialist society. His assertion that "in a socialist society wage policy is directed from the top" is ridiculous because the movement of wages in a socialist society is subordinated to definite laws that are inseparably tied to the laws of socialist expansion of reproduction and accumulation. His assumption of the possibility of "uniform wage reductions for every class of labour" in a socialist society is absurd. Those same laws of the movement of wages in socialist society that Keynes tried to sweep aside determine the systematic growth of wages and of the material living standard of the workers simultaneously with the extension of reproduction. These laws are just as inevitable as those of capitalist reproduction that determine the relative and absolute impoverishment of the worker.[30]

On page 271 Keynes indicated his preference for rising wages and stable prices for the long-run period. This preference produced this comment:

This is one of the clearest examples of the shamelessness of Keynesian apologetics. It appears as if by means of an "insignificant" reform, namely the stabilization of wages in the short-run period (i.e., forbid-

29. *Ibid.*, p. 186.   30. *Ibid.*, p. 259.

ding them to fall during a depression) and the gradual increase of wages in the long run, one can altogether liquidate crises and guarantee unending growth of the economy. However, the "insignificant" reform presented is in essence a completely fantastic proposal. The absolute and relative impoverishment of the working class is in itself an inevitable result of the general law of capitalist accumulation and nothing can be changed as long as the capitalists own the means of production. In connection with this one ought to remember the words of Comrade Stalin: "If capitalism . . . were to give the profit . . . to the systematic increase of the material standards of the workers and peasants, then there would be no crises. But then capitalism would not be capitalism" (*Voprosy Leninizma*, 10th ed., p. 35).[31]

In his last chapter, Keynes mentioned "the common will, embodied in the policy of the State."[32] The editor placed an asterisk after the "common will" and remarked in his footnote: "Read— will of the ruling class."[33] In this chapter Keynes also said: "But beyond this no obvious case is made out for a system of State Socialism which would embrace most of the economic life of the community."[34] Here the editor placed an asterisk after "State Socialism" and told the reader: "Read—state capitalism."[35]

The above list of remarks could be classified as subjective and strongly tinged with the political views of the editor. However, not all the editorial remarks fall into this category. In regard to the supply of labor as a function of real wages (*The General Theory*, pp. 8–9), the editor remarked: "Here Keynes's pen clearly slipped. Obviously, following from the above, it should be 'if the supply of labor is a function only of the real wage' and so on."[36] Another example was on page 166 in regard to "convert deferred command over specific goods into immediate command over goods in general," the editor reversed Keynes: "Here Keynes obviously made a mistake. Proceeding from the course of his discussion, it obviously should be: 'Convert deferred command over goods in general into immediate command over specific goods.' "[37] And on page 226 the

31. *Ibid.*, pp. 263–264.
32. Keynes, *The General Theory*, p. 377.
33. Keins, *Teoriya*, p. 363.
34. Keynes, *The General Theory*, p. 378.
35. Keins, *Teoriya*, p. 365.
36. *Ibid.*, p. 7.   37. *Ibid.*, p. 158.

phrase "and of money that its yield is *nil*" gave rise to this editorial clarification: "In the sense of yielding production or direct services."[38]

The editor assisted his Russian reader by a translation of all the italicized words and phrases. He identified their language (i.e., Latin or French) and gave the Russian equivalent. He also saw fit to explain and expand on a good many English words and terms. For example, he located Throgmorton Street and explained bears and bulls, overdraft, and euthanasia for his readers. He also identified the particular war Keynes was discussing, and took no chance that his readers might confuse the English poet Alexander Pope, whose father Keynes had mentioned, with the Pope in Rome.

There were a few omissions in the translation, and these could charitably be called inadvertent slips if they were of a random character. But a review of them revealed a definite pattern that led to a suspicion they were deliberate. For instance, the footnote on page 349 of *The General Theory*, in which Keynes referred to the International Labor Office as showing appreciation for full employment policies, was omitted in the Russian translation.[39] However, the largest cut was reserved for Silvio Gesell. The Soviet translation stopped after this part of the sentence found on page 353 of *The General Theory*: "It is convenient to mention at this point the strange, unduly neglected prophet Silvio Gesell (1862–1930) . . ." and began again with this sentence found on page 355: "Gesell's specific contribution to the theory of money and interest is as follows."[40] Blyumin, it will be recalled, had mentioned him in his introductory article. Yet the editor omitted the short biography of Gesell that Keynes offered in his book. Keynes had these thoughts regarding Gesell's book; presumably the Soviets found them unacceptable since they appeared to offer an alternative to Marxism:

The purpose of this book as a whole may be described as the establishment of an anti-Marxian socialism, a reaction against *laissez-faire* built on theoretical foundations totally unlike those of Marx in being based on a repudiation instead of on an acceptance of the classical hypotheses, and on an unfettering of competition instead of its abolition.

38. *Ibid.*, p. 219.
39. *Ibid.*, p. 339.
40. *Ibid.*, p. 342.

I believe that the future will learn more from the spirit of Gesell than from that of Marx. The preface to *The Natural Economic Order* will indicate to the reader, if he will refer to it, the moral quality of Gesell. The answer to Marxism is, I think, to be found along the lines of this preface.[41]

In his final chapter Keynes pronounced on individualism, personal liberty, and personal choice (page 380), but the editor omitted this significant observation: "and the loss of which individualism is the greatest of all losses of the homogeneous or totalitarian state."[42] Likewise, Keynes's statement on page 381, "The authoritarian state systems of to-day seem to solve the problem of unemployment at the expense of efficiency and of freedom," was not found in the Russian translation.[43] However, the rest of the paragraph, in which Keynes continues: "It is certain that the world will not much longer tolerate the unemployment which . . . is associated—and, in my opinion, inevitably associated—with present-day capitalistic individualism," is left in; thus the Soviet reader is given the totally erroneous impression it is capitalistic individualism alone that Keynes criticized. The editor's sensitivity to the words "authoritarian state systems" and his subsequent omission of them is in itself an admission of their striking applicability to the Stalinist regime.

With the introductory article by Blyumin and the editor's comments and omissions, one would have imagined that the work was rendered relatively innocuous to the Soviet reader. But this evidently was not the case. The translation was reviewed by V. Volodin, subsequently the author of a whole work on Keynes and his theory, in an article entitled "The False Theory of Keynes."[44] In Volodin's article, Blyumin, the editor Movshovich, the translator Lyubimov, and even the publishing house were sharply taken to task for their poor work.[45]

41. Keynes, *The General Theory*, p. 355.
42. Keins, *Teoriya*, p. 367.   43. *Ibid.*, p. 368.
44. V. Volodin, "Lzheteoriya Keinsa," *Voprosy Ekonomiki*, 1950, No. 1, pp. 108–114.
45. However, the translator has subsequently been vindicated. In a more recent Soviet textbook on economic translation, Professor Lyubimov was the only economist to be publicly acknowledged for his advice by the authors (S. N. Andrianov and L. N. Sorokina, *Textbook of Economic Translation*, Moscow, 1961, p. 6).

Volodin's article contained his own review of *The General Theory* as well. Bourgeois economic theory, he stated, was in a state of crisis, and the bourgeoisie had ordered their "hired, learned hands," the bourgeois economists, to think up various measures to save capitalism. This order was in addition to the standing order of whitewashing the capitalist system at which, in Volodin's opinion, they were so adept. As a result, plans following a definite line were submitted to battle against crisis, unemployment, socialism, democracy, and revolutionary force. Volodin found that: "The clearest outline of this line of contemporary bourgeois political economy appears in the activity of the English bourgeois economist Keynes, the author of the book under review."[46] Volodin recalled that Lenin had given an "exhaustive and murderous description" of Keynes's political activities.

Volodin found that the book under review "consisted of false and deliberately confused reasoning, and was published deceivingly as a so-called 'general theory.' It was based on old, well-known vulgar-idealistic economic views."[47] He was severe with Keynes's ideas on the trade cycle and singled out for comment some choice sentences from Keynes on the hysteria, nerves, and digestions of businessmen. According to Volodin, Keynes had approached "the herculean pillars of absurdity" with this sort of analysis and he wondered if "one could find a better illustration of the stagnation of contemporary vulgar political economy than these words of Keynes."[48]

Volodin alleged that Keynes had been forced to put one of the most important principles of bourgeois economy, laissez faire, to rest. As a result, Keynes had enlisted the aid of the state to help save capitalism. Now the bourgeois state, according to Volodin, did everything possible to aid the capitalists and harm the workers. The state would not even stop short of war to preserve capitalism. "In such a manner, the ideological justification of imperialist war and expansion have their 'proper' place in the 'general theory' of Keynes."[49] Volodin noted that the Americans were especially fond of Keynes and had used his theory to support their reactionary ex-

46. Volodin, *Voprosy Ekonomiki*, 1950, No. 1, p. 108.
47. *Ibid.*
48. *Ibid.*, p. 109.   49. *Ibid.*, p. 112.

pansionist policies. He was sure, however, that all this effort would result in failure:

The attempts of the ruling classes whose capitalist system has outlived its age and of their learned lackeys to find a solution to the ever-increasing contradictions of capitalism by means of further encroachment on the living standards of the workers, of the establishment of fascist systems, and of unleashing wars will inevitably summon only the quickening final destruction of the capitalist method of production.[50]

Throughout this lengthy review article, Volodin vented his own views and interpretation of *The General Theory*. In his final section, however, he returned to the merits of the translation. He had this to say:

This publication of the "work" of Keynes in the Soviet Union should have acquainted the public with the contemporary methods of the apologists of capitalism. It was the responsibility of the publishers to provide an introductory article to unmask Keynesianism as the ideological weapon of monopoly capital. However, the introductory article to the Russian translation of Keynes's book, *The General Theory of Employment, Interest and Money*, was written by Professor I. G. Blyumin and suffers from elements of pseudo-academicism and objectivism. Expounding in detail the contents of the Keynesian chatter, Professor Blyumin does not subject it to sharp party-type criticism. He insufficiently uncovers the real content of those measures that Keynes produces under the democratic masks of the fight against crises and unemployment, and does not unmask the conscious distortion by Keynes of the role of the bourgeois state as one of the most important links in the Keynesian scheme. I. Blyumin calls on practically no facts of contemporary capitalist activity to unmask the apologetic apparatus of Keynes. Professor Blyumin merely scatters statements about in his article that Keynesian apologetics reflect the ideology of monopolistic capital and that they serve to justify the strengthening of the development of state-monopoly capitalism and that they pursue the aim of encroaching on the living standards of the working class.

And the work of the editor, G. Movshovich, cannot satisfy the Soviet reader. Movshovich found no time to supply comments to a series of pages that were filled with praises for the contemporary capitalist system along with vile slander on the socialist system of the Soviet Union.

50. *Ibid.*, p. 113.

Finally, one cannot satisfactorily commend the translation of the book. As a consequence of the inadequate literary treatment in the Russian text there are noticeable traces of the English structure. As a result, the sharply confused expository style of Keynes was even more exaggerated in the Russian translation.

Inadmissible negligence begins with the title page in which the reader to his surprise finds that the book was translated from the 1935 edition whereas the first English edition appeared in 1936. In the translation there are also many other inaccuracies.

The defects that were permitted in the publication of this book under review should serve as a sharp signal for the State Publishing House for Foreign Langauges.[51]

Volodin's extremist attitude can be explained, in part, by the times. He wrote his review later, and events like Zhdanov's criticism and the Varga controversy had taken their effect. His performance was a typical example of Soviet economic analysis at the height of the cold war. The translation of Keynes plus the harsh political environment led to further critical attacks on his work, which will be considered next.

51. *Ibid.*, pp. 113–114.

V. *Keynes and the Cold War*

The translation of *The General Theory* into Russian made possible numerous publications on Keynes and his theory. The works dealt with the major tenets of *The General Theory* and were sharply critical of it. This is not altogether surprising when these works are placed in the context of the times. The period under review begins with the harsh atmosphere prior to Stalin's death in 1953. The pronouncements of Zhdanov together with the various political "affairs" such as the doctors' plot had their effect on Soviet scholarship. Nor were the unsettling struggles for Soviet leadership after the death of Stalin helpful to Soviet political economists.

The intensity of the cold war continued for a number of years after Stalin's death, during which time Keynes and his theory received widespread critical attention and the literature on him became voluminous. Representative examples of this criticism will be considered and analyzed for the period prior to the famous Twentieth Party Congress of 1956.

Among the first writers to mention Keynes was the Soviet economist A. Shapiro in an article entitled "The Growth of Unemployment in the Capitalist Countries in the Postwar Period."[1] Here Shapiro gave an alarming picture of unemployment in the Western countries:

> The colossal growth of chronic mass unemployment in the capitalist countries after World War II exposed the bankruptcy of the various theories of "full employment" that were invented by bourgeois economic thought. All the apologists of the capitalist system—both the stagnationists and the anti-stagnationists, the advocates of the notorious "regulation" and the opponents of it—consider that a significant percentile of unemployment is altogether necessary, as Keynes expressed it: "for the orderly functioning of the economy."[2]

1. A. Shapiro, "Rost bezrabotitsy v kapitalisticheskikh stranakh v poslevoennyi period," *Voprosy Ekonomiki*, 1949, No. 9, pp. 76–91.
2. *Ibid.*, p. 89.

Shapiro continued the theme of necessary unemployment for capitalist systems and quoted Hansen and Beveridge as Keynesian representatives who advocated a certain percentage of unemployment. In answer to his own question as to the necessity for unemployment, Shapiro quoted Keynes, who had openly admitted that a necessary percentage of unemployment would prevent the disturbing aspects of wage increases. Keynes and his accomplices were found to sow false illusions with their theories to reduce unemployment, and Shapiro predicted their failure in dealing with this problem.

Soviet writers strongly objected to the view that there were possibly two or even more interpretations of Keynes. Western Marxist writers of the period gave various interpretations of Keynes, but all were unacceptable to the Soviets. For example, V. Seregin reviewed *The Economic Crisis and the Cold War*[3] in an article entitled "Monopoly Capital of the USA—Instigator of War."[4] After the usual introduction on the necessity of wars for American imperialism, Seregin proceeded to discuss the policy behind the warmongering activity of the imperialists:

The book points out that the policy of the "regulated economy," which is conducted by the ruling circles of the USA, is based on the "theory" of Keynes—that apologist of the capitalist system. The authors correctly criticize the unscientific "theory" of Keynes, but at the same time they attempt to establish the availability of two different views of Keynesianism—reformist and reactionary—and subscribe various progressive goals to the first view. . . .

Not satisfied with the division of Keynesians into reformers and reactionaries, the book points out that there is still an "in-between group," composed of such elements as Americans for Democratic Action, right-wing social democrats, conservative trade unions . . . which "support the measures of the reformist Keynesians but at the same time give serious support to the reactionary program of armaments. . . ."[5]

Seregin strongly objected to these categories and interpretations of Keynes: "In reality there are no 'two Keyneses'—the reformist

---

3. J. Allen and D. Wilkerson, eds., *The Economic Crisis and the Cold War* (New York, 1949).

4. V. Seregin, "Monopolisticheskii kapital SShA—podzhigatel voiny," *Bolshevik*, 1950, No. 4, pp. 73–80.

5. *Ibid.*, p. 76.

and the reactionary. Even Lenin gave an exhaustive description of Keynes, this god of the financial oligarchy, as a 'bourgeois philistine, an avowed opponent of bolshevism.' "[6] In the opinion of Seregin, there was only one Keynes, and his theory was explained in this manner:

Keynesianism—this is the "theory" of monopoly capital in the period of the general crisis of capitalism when capitalism has lost its former "stability" and when its very days are numbered. In their convulsive search to save capitalism, which has outlived its age, the financial oligarchy have seized upon the "theory" of Keynes, whose conclusions justify the "foundation" of the rule of state-monopoly capitalism, and its incursion on the standard of living of the working class, and the unleashing of imperialist wars.[7]

It is interesting to note that William Z. Foster, the leader of the American Communist party, had two interpretations of Keynesianism at this time:

The big monopolists who own our country and our government are quite aware of this impossible marketing situation, and they are full of alarm as to the economic future. . . . Their basic problem is to "fill the gap" between overdeveloped production and the lagging purchasing power of the people of this and other countries. This they don't intend to try to do in any major sense in the manner that the liberal Keynesians propose, namely, through government works, raising the workers' living standards, establishing social security, and the like. They have their own reactionary version of Keynesianism. They propose to fill the economic gap between production and consumption primarily by building up a big economy, which will feed American industry with a score or two billions of dollars in munitions orders every year.[8]

This view, which again admitted the possibility of varying interpretations of Keynesianism, was severely criticized by M. Rubinshtein in an article entitled "The Unmasking of Bourgeois Economic Science by Lenin."[9] Rubinshtein took this passage from Lenin as his text:

6. *Ibid.*   7. *Ibid.*
8. William Z. Foster, *The Twilight of Capitalism* (New York, 1949), p. 34.
9. M. Rubinshtein, "Razoblachenie Leninym burzhuaznoi ekonomicheskoi nauki," *Voprosy Ekonomiki*, 1950, No. 4, pp. 19–36.

the social position of professors in bourgeois society is such that only those who sell their science to the interests of capital and only those who agree to speak the most unbelievable absurdities, shameless nonsense, and rubbish are admitted to this profession. The bourgeoisie will forgive the professors all this only if they will busy themselves with the "destruction" of socialism.[10]

Rubinshtein maintained that this description by Lenin was still applicable, for bourgeois professors and the "yellow press" were spreading slanders against the Soviet Union and once again were proclaiming the "final destruction" of socialism. According to Marx, the superficiality of bourgeois economic thought could be measured by its great thinkers, and Rubinshtein noted that Keynes had been given this honor by the representatives of bourgeois political economy: "They try to present the English economist Keynes as a 'great thinker' and prophet of bourgeois economic thought of our times in the USA and England."[11]

Rubinshtein found Keynes's theory to be a mixed-up concoction of theories that had been discredited long ago. Keynes was accused of repeating Sismondi on the theory of underconsumption. Keynes's magical formula to save capitalism by pyramid-building, earthquakes, and even wars could only bring delight to the war-oriented industrial monopolists. Rubinshtein contended that this policy would strengthen the exploitation of the workers, whose income would be confiscated by the state and used to finance military preparations. In this respect Lenin had been accurate in his description of Keynes as long ago as 1920:

In 1920 Lenin called Keynes an "English philistine, an avowed bourgeois, a ruthless opponent of bolshevism." Later Keynes became an open ideologist of imperialist wars. This is the fashionable prophet of bourgeois economic science whom the monopolistic press attempts to present as a "great thinker." Hundreds of learned servants of monopoly capital made a career for themselves by adapting the "abstract" theories of Keynes to the concrete problems of the economic policies of monopolies, and are serving the monopolies in the state apparatus.[12]

---

10. *Ibid.*, p. 23. The reference to Lenin was: Lenin, *Sochineniya*, XVII, 566.
11. Rubinshtein, *Voprosy Ekonomiki*, 1950, No. 4, p. 31.
12. *Ibid.*, p. 31–32.

Rubinshtein recalled that Keynesian theories were popular in Hitlerite Germany. Likewise at the present time, the "fascist American pretenders" had seized upon Keynes in their bid for world rule. According to Rubinshtein, this interpretation represented the true Keynesianism; in his conclusion he dismissed the possibility of any other interpretation of Keynes:

Legends have been created by some American and Western European economists about the availability of "two Keyneses"—the reactionary and the reformist—and that Keynesianism has some sort of progressive side or purpose to it. This only enables the spread of harmful illusions about the possibility of the bourgeois state's introducing social reforms and transforming monopoly capitalism into some sort of "progressive capitalism" in the period of the general crisis of capitalism. It is well known that the contemporary state apparatus of bourgeois power completely and unreservedly serves the interests of monopoly capital and is directed to the preparation of imperialist wars and to the crushing of the working class and its organizations.[13]

During this period of the two Keyneses controversy, a dissertation on *The General Theory* was accepted by the Institute of Economics of the Academy of Sciences of the USSR. The defense of his dissertation by V. S. Volodin, the author of the article on Keynes discussed in the previous chapter, was published in an abbreviated form in the *Bulletin of the Academy of Sciences.*[14] The committee was composed of the following distinguished Soviet economists: I. N. Dvorkin, L. B. Alter, and I. G. Blyumin were the official opponents; P. A. Khromov, G. A. Kozlov, I. A. Trakhtenberg, E. S. Varga, and the academic director of the dissertation, Professor N. A. Tsagolov, were the discussants at the defense, which took place on July 1, 1949.

Volodin opened his defense with a brief review of the dissertation and its purpose. He maintained that the division of the world into two systems and the construction of socialism in the USSR had disturbed the bourgeois economists. Further, the contradictions in the capitalist system that resulted in crises, unemployment, and revolutionary activity on the part of the masses had sharpened to a point

13. *Ibid.*, p. 32.
14. Akademiya Nauk SSSR, "Kritika knigi Keinsa *Obshchaya teoriya zanyatosti, protsenta i deneg," Izvestiya Akademii Nauk SSSR*, Otdelenie Ekonomiki i Prava, 1950, No. 1, pp. 52–57.

where bourgeois economists had to seek a new defense of the capitalist system. And it was his contention that the fullest expression of this reorganization in the apologetics of capitalism was to be found in Keynes.

Volodin took the familiar Marxist approach that Keynes in reality had offered a program for the further encroachment on the living standards of the workers by the monopoly capitalists even though he had taken refuge in demagogic slogans on the improvement of capitalism and the liquidation of crises and unemployment. The danger of Keynes's program, Volodin continued, was that it diverted the workers from the revolutionary struggle—"the only possible path for the final liberation from capitalist slavery."[15]

Volodin argued that Keynesianism had become widespread among reformists and that the unmasking of this theory constituted one of the urgent tasks of Soviet economic science. As a result, he had chosen a critical analysis of *The General Theory* as the subject of his dissertation:

The Keynesian apologetics are the convenient ideological weapon of modern reformism. The leaders of the right-wing socialists and the reformist trade unions in their infamous activity of betraying the interests of the working class and in their lackey-like obsequiousness to monopoly capital fully exploit Keynesian ideas.

The unmasking of the real class content of the apologetics of Keynes is one of the urgent tasks of our economic science.

And this aroused me to select as the theme of my dissertation the criticism of the basic work of Keynes, *The General Theory of Employment, Interest and Money.*[16]

Volodin listed the chapter headings of his dissertation and said his work had drawn heavily on available Soviet sources, mainly journal articles, which had dealt with various aspects of Keynes and his theory. However, in his opinion, the majority of these Soviet works had failed to give the necessary emphasis to exposing the real essence of Keynes, which was hidden behind the slogans of eliminating crises and unemployment:

The chatter of the possibility of liquidating unemployment and economic crises in capitalism serves Keynes only as a smoke screen with the help of which he attempts to hide the real content of his especially

15. *Ibid.*, p. 53.   16. *Ibid.*, p. 52.

anti-people's program directed pointedly against the working class. The unmasking of the conscious distortions by Keynes of the role of the contemporary bourgeois state is the most important requisite in explaining the real content of the Keynesian program of the transition to the so-called "regulated" capitalism, which in itself is nothing other than a new charlatan project for the notorious "organized capitalism."[17]

Volodin contended that the reorganization that bourgeois political economy found necessary resulted in changes in its content as well as in its methods. Certain tenets like the existence of only voluntary unemployment had to be discarded in the face of reality. The new content was that intervention on the part of the state in the economy would result in the elimination of unemployment and crises. This course, Volodin added, only benefited the monopolists at the expense of the working masses. The new dogma of state intervention in the economy and the methods to propagate it widely led to the distraction of the proletariat from its revolutionary tasks. Volodin then reviewed the Keynesian influence in England, Germany, and the United States. He concluded, as might be expected, that these attempts to adopt the Keynesian theory would end in failure and that the Soviet Union provided the best proof of the only method of solving unemployment and economic crises.

The state "regulation" put into practice by the ruling circles in the postwar period approximates closer and closer in its character the type of so-called "regulation" that was openly peculiar to the fascist form of rule by finance capital.

There is no doubt that the similar nature of the method of "regulation" will bring the USA imperialists to the same sad ending to which Hitlerite Germany came in its time.

The socialist system of the Soviet Union is the best refutation of all the Keynesian apologetics of capitalism and is proof that the only method of liquidating crises, unemployment, and all the other inevitable fellow travelers of capitalism is the destruction of the latter.[18]

Professor Tsagolov, the director of the dissertation, spoke next on the basic points of Volodin's work. In his opinion Volodin had taken the existing criticism of Keynes and developed it further and more fully. Essentially, Volodin had developed and analyzed two existing

17. *Ibid.*, p. 53.　　　　18. *Ibid.*, p. 55.

propositions, namely that Keynes's theoretical system was an original and new form of capitalist apologetics and that his system was aggressive in that it was a weapon against the working class and socialism. Volodin had carried out his plan of work in an orderly and serious manner, Tsagolov continued, and this was the first attempt to criticize and also to unmask Keynes analytically and systematically. Tsagolov concluded that Volodin deserved to be awarded the degree, and added: "The work of Comrade Volodin is original and deserves publication."[19]

Dvorkin, Alter, and Blyumin were designated as the official opponents, and they had the unenviable task of criticizing the dissertation. Dvorkin's criticisms were mild and constructive. In his opinion, the theory of employment was the essence of the Keynesian doctrine, and its central feature was its wage policy. All this was well hidden, but Volodin had exposed Keynes better than those Soviet economists who generally treated wages separately from employment. However, Volodin had failed to emphasize the relationship between interest and profit. Dvorkin also said that there should be no mention of socialism in connection with Keynes. Apart from these criticisms, Dvorkin agreed that Volodin had revealed the real essence of the role of the state in the capitalist system and that he had properly evaluated Keynes as the worst enemy of the working class. Dvorkin thought Volodin fully deserved to be awarded his degree. Blyumin and Alter offered no opposition and concurred with Dvorkin that Volodin's work had completely fulfilled the requirements for the degree. One might perhaps have expected a firmer stand on the part of Blyumin in particular, who could have taken this opportunity to defend himself against Volodin's earlier criticisms of his introductory article on the Russian translation of Keynes.

It appeared that only Varga had any doubts as to whether the dissertation met the official standards. His reasons were as follows:

> The question above all is whether the analysis of a single book and the criticism of its theme are sufficient for a candidate's dissertation. Obviously, the book of Keynes has great significance, but if we take this path, then one can offer a dissertation on Mitchell's book, on Hansen's

19. *Ibid.*

book, on Cassel's book, or Hilferding's book, on Renner's book, and so forth, which are just as harmful as Keynes's book.

Judging by its abstract, the dissertation assigns to Keynes a new method of demagoguery. The candidate says that Keynes is a specialist in creating an illusion among the working masses of the possibility of improving capitalism by a reformist path in order to distract these same workers from the revolutionary struggle. This is in no way novel. All reformism follows this goal and hundreds of bourgeois economists are doing this same thing. . . .

Besides, I consider that the dissertation is too theoretical and that its political aspect is insufficiently expressed.[20]

Khromov came to Volodin's defense and maintained that the analysis of a single work was completely acceptable for a dissertation. This was especially so in this case as Keynes's work had been evaluated by bourgeois economists as their contemporary version of *Capital*. There were precedents for accepting a single work, and Khromov concluded: "The dissertation of Comrade Volodin is the first instance in which a young academic worker had the courage to challenge with devasting criticism the most prominent contemporary bourgeois economist."[21]

Trakhtenberg and Kozlov also opposed Varga. Volodin's work had met the standards in their opinion and they gave it their approval. Trakhtenberg, however, thought that Volodin failed to develop sufficiently the English background of Keynes. The discussion was closed, and Volodin in his concluding address could be considered to have answered the criticisms of Varga and Trakhtenberg satisfactorily. The professional committee accepted Volodin's dissertation and awarded his degree.

The foregoing is evidence that the Soviets were becoming increasingly interested in Keynes and fearful of the spread of his influence. They now evaluated Keynes as the chief ideologist of the bourgeoisie. A significant example of this estimate of Keynes was an article entitled "Keynesianism—the Ideology of the Reactionary Imperialist Bourgeoisie,"[22] by A. I. Kochetkov, which appeared in the *Bulletin of the Academy of Sciences*.

Kochetkov began his article by explaining the division among the

20. *Ibid.*, p. 56.   21. *Ibid.*, p. 57.
22. A. I. Kochetkov, "Keinsianstvo—ideologiya reaktsionnoi imperialisticheskoi

non-Marxist economists: "Contemporary reactionary bourgeois economists are divided into two schools: Keynesians and anti-Keynesians. This division is of a purely formal and semantic character as both schools are reactionary and reflect the interests of the magnates of finance capital."[23] Kochetkov proceeded to quote Marx on the point that bourgeois economists were open defenders of the bourgeoisie. This was followed by several references to Lenin on the subject of bourgeois economists, namely that non-Marxist political economy after Marx only existed to deceive the petty bourgeoisie and that one should neither trust nor believe a single word of any professor of bourgeois political economy on the subject of a general theory of political economy, though these professors could make valuable contributions in special, limited areas. With this support, Kochetkov returned to the theme of the two schools and gave his reasons for the dominance of the Keynesian school:

The economic and political ideas of both schools are reactionary, pseudo-scientific, and directed against the vital interests of the working class and all toilers. Presently, however, the most harmful, dangerous, and obstructive to the revolutionary struggle of the working masses in the capitalist countries for the socialist revolution is the school of the English reactionary economist Keynes, for it conceals its pseudo-scientific ideas in social demagoguery and serves as the main ideological base of the expansionist Anglo-American aggressive bloc.[24]

Kochetkov reviewed briefly the life of Keynes and the publication of *The General Theory*. This work, said Kochetkov, followed the crises of 1929–1933 and was written to fulfil the command of the monopolists who demanded more refined methods to justify the exploitation of the masses. In the opinion of Kochetkov, Keynes had succeeded in serving the monopolists. Kochetkov called on his fellow economists to unmask Keynes: "Therefore, Soviet economists must without ceasing unmask the reactionary and pseudo-scientific economic ideas and practical proposals of Keynes and his school, and show that Keynesianism is the reactionary ideology of the imperialist bourgeoisie."[25]

---

burzhuazii," *Izvestiya Akademii Nauk SSSR*, Otdelenie Ekonomiki i Prava, 1950, No. 6, pp. 425–439.
23. *Ibid.*, p. 425.
24. *Ibid.*, p. 427.   25. *Ibid.*, p. 429.

Kochetkov maintained that Keynes had created no revolution in political economy and that he was even more reactionary than, say, Marshall, and Malthus. Keynesianism, continued Kochetkov, was the ideological basis for fascism and cosmopolitanism, and Keynesians were the worst enemies of the working class. Keynesian methodology was based on subjective idealism, obscurantism, and religious hypocrisy. Keynes had refused to consider the capitalist mode of production and had chosen psychological factors to explain the moving forces of the capitalist system. He had retained Marshall's teaching on costs and refused to acknowledge the labor theory of value. He had recognized some shortcomings of the capitalist system but still considered it as the only progressive and irreplaceable economic system.

Kochetkov thought that the theory of employment was at the heart of the Keynesian system. He listed the concepts that explained the level of employment and then dismissed these concepts as devices only to intensify the exploitation of the workers:

The real meaning and significance of this confused reasoning of Keynes is for the purpose of realizing a systematic increase of the marginal efficiency of capital, i.e., the rate of profits, at the expense of lowering real wages and of increasing the intensification of labor because, according to Keynes, the increase of demand, investment, and employment can happen solely by means of an uninterrupted lowering of the real wages of the workers and the toiling masses. Keynes himself cynically says: "An increase of employment can take place only under the condition of lowering real wages." The intervention of the bourgeois state in the economic life is only necessary, in Keynes's opinion, in order that the state guarantee a high marginal efficiency of capital, i.e., a high rate of profit for the capitalist monopolies. The constant lowering of real wages and the systematic increasing of the intensification of labor for the sake of the unceasing increase of the rate of profit for monopolies—such is the aim of the theory of employment of Keynes.[26]

Kochetkov gave figures to prove that real wages had fallen in England and the United States in the postwar period, whereas profits had increased two to three times in England and five times in America. The figures given were designated "official" and the only reference

26. *Ibid.*, p. 431.

was that they had been corrected by the Oxford Statistical Institute. Such were the results, maintained Kochetkov, of the inflationary Keynesian policies. Furthermore, Kochetkov emphasized that unemployment had not disappeared, and he provided his readers with statistics on this point. Lastly, Stalin was quoted as saying that not a single capitalist would ever agree to the complete liquidation of unemployment.

Kochetkov noticed that the Keynesians "chatter" a great deal about the possibility of overcoming economic crises and about the possibility of planning within the framework of capitalism. This involved the intervention by the state to plan demand, investment, and the rate of interest in order to increase employment. Kochetkov believed the purpose of these ideas was to deceive the workers into believing that their position could improve under capitalism. As a result, the Keynesian ideology was accepted by reformist groups:

> That is why the Keynesian arguments about the possibility of eliminating economic crises and unemployment and about the possibility of planning the economy within the framework of capitalism were seized upon with the greatest pleasure by the right-wing social democrats and the trade-union bureaucrats in all the capitalist countries, especially in England and the United States. The right-wing social democrats and socialists have placed the pseudo-scientific reactionary ideas of Keynes at the foundation of their ideological work among the workers, maintaining that Lord Keynes found the key for the peaceful transition of capitalism into socialism. Fulfilling the will of English and American imperialism, the right-wing laborites have taken the reactionary economic ideas of Keynes as the basis for their economic policies.[27]

Kochetkov, like others before him, recalled that Keynesianism had also served the fascists. Hitlerite Germany accepted Keynes's theory for the basis of its economic system even before it was accepted in England. The bourgeois classical school, Kochetkov explained, was still predominant at that time in England. But he reminded his readers that the fascist system collapsed and predicted a similar fate for others following Keynesianism. He quoted Walter Lippmann as evidence of Keynesian influence: "Thus, in the *New York Herald Tribune* even as far back as November 25, 1947, Wal-

27. *Ibid.*, p. 434.

ter Lippmann openly declared that the communists who were waiting for the appearance of an economic crisis in the USA are mistaken and can correct their mistakes by reading John Maynard Keynes's book."[28]

Kochetkov contended that planning could not take place in the capitalist system. Stalin was quoted to this effect for emphasis. The intervention of the state in the capitalist system, continued Kochetkov, only provided super-profits for the capitalists and increased the misery of the workers:

Keynesianism is the worst enemy of bolshevism, people's democracy, and humanity. The assertions of the right-wing social democrats, socialists, and laborites that Keynesian economic ideas and practical proposals have as their aim the elimination of crises and unemployment and the gradual growth of capitalism into socialism are for the sheer deceit of the working masses.[29]

Kochetkov called on his fellow Marxists to unmask Keynes:

The most important task of the Marxists is to unmask to the end the reactionary economic and political ideas of Keynes and his followers, and to show by concrete examples who will benefit by these ideas and who will suffer exceedingly great harm, and to show that Keynesianism is the ideology of the reactionary imperialist bourgeoisie.[30]

In the same breath Kochetkov maintained that bourgeois economic science was in crisis and, in fact, had ceased to be a science. Keynesianism was evidence of this sickness. On the other hand, he concluded, the Soviet Union had proved the superiority of Marxism, and he quoted Molotov to the effect that all roads lead to communism.

Even more significant than the above was a later article by I. Kuzminov in *Bolshevik* entitled "Keynes—the Ideologist of Imperialist Reaction and War."[31] Since *Bolshevik* (later *Kommunist*) is the theoretical and political journal of the Central Committee of the Communist party, this article can be viewed as the official assessment of Keynes.

Kuzminov began with the division of the world into two systems

28. *Ibid.*, p. 438.
29. *Ibid.*   30. *Ibid.*, p. 439.
31. I. Kuzminov, "Keins—ideolog imperialisticheskoi reaktsii i voiny," *Bolshevik*, 1951, No. 19, pp. 39–52.

—capitalist and socialist. As a result of this division, the capitalist system was not the only system in existence and its ideology had to be reconstructed and oriented to the new conditions, i.e., the appearance of socialism. Further, according to Kuzminov, unemployment remained a serious problem. Also the militarization of the economy and wars became even more important sources of profits for the monopolists. All the above led the monopolists to order a new invention for the regulation of the economy in their interests from their learned servants, the bourgeois economists:

This order of the monopolist bourgeoisie was fulfilled by the English economist Keynes . . . . Keynes became the real idol of the modern apologists of the capitalist system. With the publication of this book Keynes ushered in the beginning of a new school among bourgeois economists that was named Keynesian. Keynesianism is the ideological product of the general crises of capitalism.[32]

Keynes had admitted to some of the "sores" of capitalism in his book, Kuzminov explained, only to gain his own end to deceive the working masses: "The book of Keynes, written with the aim of praising capitalism and deceiving the masses, is a product of the decay of bourgeois political economy and smells of wizardry and sorcery for a mile and is enriched with a goodly share of demagoguery."[33]

Kuzminov thought Keynes had been afraid of the word "unemployment" and had preferred therefore to discuss the problem in terms of the quantity of employment. Kuzminov reviewed the Keynesian concept concerning aggregate demand which determined the level of employment. The Keynesian edifice, in the opinion of Kuzminov, was based on his fundamental psychological law that not all additional income would be spent. Kuzminov found this law defective.

The famous flaw in aggregate demand arose from this law. Keynes, who formulated and thought up this "basic psychological law," attempts to whitewash capitalism and to relieve it of the responsibility for unemployment. The trouble, so to speak, is not with capitalism but in the psychology of the people who are always induced to save more than they spend out of additional income.[34]

32. *Ibid.*, p. 40.
33. *Ibid.*, p. 41.   34. *Ibid.*

Keynes, Kuzminov added, made the assumption that workers saved a considerable part of their income that did not enter into investment. Hence difficulties arose in the Keynesian scheme, and it was necessary to outline a program to increase investment. Kuzminov discussed the inducement to invest and future prospects of investment. He maintained that there could be no knowledge of the future in the capitalist system because of the anarchy of production relations. Kuzminov claimed Keynes had known of this uncertainty and even admitted it. Since the future was uncertain and since businessmen fluctuated between extremes of optimism and pessimism, Kuzminov thought it very clear why Keynes had introduced the "firm" hand of state interference in the economy. This Keynesian device, explained Kuzminov, was in the interests of the monopolists at the expense of the workers.

Kuzminov also dealt with the rate of interest in the Keynesian scheme. Keynes had wanted to control the rate of interest and to reduce it. However, Kuzminov was of the opinion that the rate of interest had fallen in the capitalist countries during the period of crisis and that unemployment remained and even increased. Likewise, rentiers had not disappeared but had even prospered. Keynes had had a definite purpose in introducing his ideas on interest, and Kuzminov put it this way: "The learned serf of the monopolist bourgeoisie attempted by demagogic chatter regarding the lowering of the rate of interest and the 'euthanasia of the rentier' to confuse his reader and distract the worker's attention from the fight against the capitalist system."[35]

Kuzminov found that the state was to do some investing as well as controlling the rate of interest. Keynes had referred to this activity as the socialization of investment, but Kuzminov maintained that this had nothing whatever to do with socialism. It was in the interests of the monopolies, a point Kuzminov illustrated by the example of the sale of industrial plants built by the government in England and the United States to private industry at a fraction of their original cost, which had been borne by the tax-paying workers. Kuzminov insisted that government investment could not relieve unemploy-

35. *Ibid.*, p. 45.

ment, since unemployment was an integral part of capitalism. The monopolists gained from such Keynesian prescriptions. Kuzminov reminded his readers that Keynes was silent on the subject of monopolies. The entire thesis of inadequate investment, Kuzminov stated, was contrary to the facts:

Proclaiming the insufficiency of investment as the reason for unemployment, Keynes proceeds from the premise of the shortage of existing basic capital to employ all the workers in production. However, this premise stands in sharp contradiction to reality. The matter is simply that in the period of the general crisis of capitalism there exists large-scale chronic underutilization of enterprises as well as chronic mass unemployment. The presence of chronic underutilization of enterprises along with unemployment cuts the ground from under the basic thesis of Keynes—as though it were entirely a matter of insufficient investment.[36]

Kuzminov summarized the Keynesian proposals to increase consumption, measures, he said, that also came from Keynes's "magic kitchen." The policy of Keynes simply amounted to the reduction of the real wages of the workers by means of inflation and increased taxation:

In the matter of lowering real wages Keynes especially underscores the role of inflation. Along with it Keynes preaches the role of the tax burden. In this manner, the "regulation of the propensity to consume" of the working class signifies in fact a program for the encroachment on the living standards of the working class.[37]

At the same time, Kuzminov said Keynes had recommended an increase of unproductive and luxury consumption. This was due to the influence of Malthus on Keynes. In fact, Kuzminov maintained that Keynes had even regarded earthquakes and wars favorably, since their effects increased unproductive consumption:

Keynes theoretically "based" the constant growth of taxes and the swelling of the government debt in capitalist countries on the goal of financing the growing military budget. "Wars," he wrote, "are the single form of large expenditures on the basis of huge loans which government leaders consider justified. . . ."

36. *Ibid.*, p. 47.   37. *Ibid.*, p. 48.

Contemporary followers of Keynes openly praise and adapt in practice the reactionary and military essence of his "theory." They "theoretically" base the rash growth of the government debt on the goals of financing war.[38]

In concluding his article, Kuzminov gave this evaluation of the Keynesian program: "As we have seen, this is a program of the state 'regulation' of the economic life in the interest of the monopolies, a program of war and reaction and a program of state-monopoly capitalism."[39] However, he stressed the point that Keynes had presented nothing new, but had only reflected what already existed from the bourgeois point of view. He again reviewed militarization, inflation, increased taxes, and growing war debts. The worker had to bear the burden and his living standard was reduced correspondingly. Kuzminov asked:

Now where is the prosperity that Keynes promised, the full employment, the riddance of those "repulsive features of capitalism"? They are nowhere! Moreover, all the contradictions of capitalism are sharpening, and the repulsive sores of capitalism are oozing distinctly in all their ugliness. . . .

In these conditions the workers and all progressive people in the capitalist countries begin more and more to understand the reactionary essence of the writings of Keynes and other "medics" of capitalism, who attempt to push nations into the abyss of a new world war. It becomes clearer all the time that the ideology of Keynesianism is the ideology of imperialist reaction and war. . . . The false assurances of Keynes about the possibility of liquidating unemployment, the anarchy of production and crises, about the possibility of planning and "full employment" in capitalism are increasingly used by the right-wing socialists to deceive the masses. . . . It is clear for all the progressive peoples in the world that the real reason for crises and unemployment is concealed in the very nature of capitalism and that the path Keynes recommends only leads to the increase in the strength of the monopolies and to the strengthening of reaction and the fostering of new wars. The unmasking of the pseudo-scientific theory of Keynes and his followers serves in the struggle for peace and democracy and against imperialist reaction and wars.[40]

38. *Ibid.*, pp. 48–49.
39. *Ibid.*, p. 52.   40. *Ibid.*

In keeping with the theme of Kuzminov's article, V. S. Volodin, the author of the dissertation on *The General Theory* discussed earlier in this chapter, wrote a book entitled *Keynes—Ideologist of Monopolistic Capital.*[41] This work may well have been his published dissertation, since, it will be recalled, the director of his dissertation had recommended its publication. It was published by the Academy of Sciences and was authorized for publication by the Institute of Economics. This book was unique in the field of Soviet political economy in that its content was based solely on Keynes and his theory. There have been many Soviet books criticizing general subjects like capitalism, unemployment, and bourgeois economic thought. Likewise a number of translations of works by foreign economists have appeared on occasion. Articles have dealt with a particular Western economist, but Volodin's work is the first and as yet the only full-length treatment devoted to a single contemporary Western bourgeois economist.

In his introduction Volodin briefly reviewed the origins and purpose of bourgeois political economy. Marx and Lenin were the references given to refute the anti-scientific bourgeois character of Western political economy. After the bourgeoisie had seized power in the nineteenth century, bourgeois political economy became a "party" science and only reflected the interests of the bourgeoisie. Volodin claimed that this trend was even more obvious today in the period of capitalism's crisis. In his opinion bourgeois political economy was thoroughly discredited. Instead of scientific economic investigation, bourgeois economists set themselves these three basic tasks:

First task—to conceal the real reasons for the sharp contradictions of contemporary capitalism, and to justify those obvious developments that are further increasing the decay of the world capitalist system . . . .

Second task—to justify ideologically the anti-people imperialist policy and action of the ruling reactionary cliques of monopoly capital within their own country and in the international arena . . . .

An important part of this task is the attempt to conceal the fact that the modern bourgeois state is subordinated to the monopolies and is

41. V. S. Volodin, *Keins—ideolog monopolisticheskogo kapitala* (Moskva, 1953). Hereinafter cited as *Keins—ideolog.*

used by the latter in the capacity of one of the most important weapons preserving the rotting foundations of capitalism . . . .

Third task—to battle against socialism and particularly scientific Marxist-Leninist ideology, the ideology of the rising communist social system. The battle is primarily against the Soviet Union, which is building the communist society, and with the people's democracies whose countries are successfully constructing socialism.[42]

To fulfil these tasks bourgeois economists continued to propound new theories to beautify capitalism. Volodin identified Keynes as the most characteristic representative of the contemporary bourgeois economists:

Keynes is a zealous defender of contemporary modern capitalism . . . .

The "discoveries" of Keynes of the so-called "regulated capitalism" are as a matter of fact nothing other than contemporary state-monopoly capitalism . . . .

He founded the beginnings of a whole school in contemporary bourgeois political economy in England and beyond her borders . . . .

Keynes is the militant ideologist of monopoly capital . . . .[43]

Volodin also found Keynes's ideas to have been propagated in Hitlerite Germany. Now Keynes was popular in the USA and England because his measures suited the monopolists. In fact, Volodin observed, these Keynesian fabrications represented the most varied forms of imperialist reaction. Followers of Keynes's ideas initiated and supported such measures as anti-labor legislation, the banning of strikes, forced arbitration, the wage freeze, and so forth. All this was against the workers, whom the Keynesians artfully deceived. Keynesianism was widespread and dangerous. Hence, Volodin had written this book to present the true Keynes: "This work which is offered to the reader as its goal to demonstrate the anti-people imperialist essence of Keynes."[44]

Volodin devoted his first chapter to the subject of Keynesianism, which he found to be a typical statement of vulgar political economy in the period of the general crisis of capitalism. Volodin maintained that Keynes had served monopoly capitalism all his life. All his works, especially *The General Theory*, had tried to prove that capi-

42. *Ibid.*, p. 5.
43. *Ibid.*, pp. 6–7.   44. *Ibid.*, p. 8.

talism was not on the threshold of destruction and that imperialism was not the final stage of capitalism. Volodin contended that Keynes had attempted to introduce a new stage of regulated capitalism. Keynes's task, he concluded, had been to save capitalism at any price. Volodin provided quotations designed to show that Keynes was hostile to the Soviet Union and that he had hoped to smash the foundations of Marxism with *The General Theory*.

After a review of Keynes's earlier publications, Volodin discussed *The General Theory*. This book was found to be the answer to the monopolist's plight following the 1929 crash. He repeated much of the earlier argument about Keynes's repudiation of laissez faire and admission of the difficulties facing capitalism only to the extent necessary to deceive the workers. He accused Keynes of faulty analysis and interpretation:

> The characteristic feature of the apologetics of Keynes is that it is based on the deliberately false interpretation of the interrelation between the sphere of production and the sphere of distribution. In fact Keynes proceeds from the assumption of the primacy of distribution in all his artificial constructions. This false contention, as it is known, is related to one of the most favored methods that is widely used all the time by the bourgeois economists of all shades of opinion from petty bourgeois "critics" of capitalism to the direct defenders of it.[45]

Volodin maintained that Keynes had chosen distribution to cover up private property. Keynes was also taken to task for introducing psychological factors that, together with the sphere of distribution, concealed the basis of capitalist production relations. Volodin challenged Keynes's assumption that consumption was the aim of all economic activity, quoting from Stalin to prove that the aim of the capitalist system was profit—and maximum profit at that.[46] Keynes had rejected the labor theory of value and presented the subjective theory value in his theory in order to conceal the exploitation of the workers.

The financial monopolists needed a reorganization of bourgeois

45. *Ibid.*, p. 21.
46. *Ibid.*, p. 23. Volodin quoted Stalin who analyzed three categories of profit: average, super, and maximum, and stated it was maximum profit that motivated monopoly capitalists. I. V. Stalin, *Ekonomicheskie problemy sotsializma v SSSR* (Moskva, 1952), p. 39.

political economy, and Volodin claimed that Keynes had fulfilled this need. In his opinion, Keynes had repudiated Say's law and laissez faire because these concepts had outgrown their usefulness. However, Volodin thought that this repudiation was not complete. In the case of Say's law:

The difference between Keynes and his predecessors, the "old-fashioned" supporters of the "theory of markets," is not one of essence. The predecessors of Keynes considered that equilibrium between supply and demand was reached automatically with the help of the spontaneously acting mechanism of capitalist competition in the market. Acting in the capacity of the ideologist of state-monopoly capitalism, Keynes claimed that "state regulation" of the economy was the necessary additional lever for the operation of the mechanism of capitalist competition that guaranteed equilibrium between supply and demand on some kind of a maximum high level that corresponded to the fullest use of material and human resources.[47]

Volodin added that Keynes had thought wages could be lowered further, whereas his predecessors had considered that wages were at their lower limits. Drawing a parallel with Keynes's position regarding Say's law, he found that Keynes had not completely repudiated the principle of laissez faire:

Keynes does not reject the principle of "laissez faire" completely but gives it a somewhat different meaning. Unlimited freedom and rights for the handful of monopolists and the complete absence of these freedoms and rights for the toiling masses—such is the real meaning of this "principle" in his view as it is in reality interpreted by Keynes.[48]

He admitted that Keynes was clever and cunning. As a result Keynes had misled "progressive" economists, who were not altogether clear as to Keynes's true position. Hence it was necessary, Volodin emphasized, to unmask Keynes. He reviewed the thesis of the so-called two views on Keynes—reformist and reactionary—and stated his conclusion firmly:

In reality a reformist version of Keynes does not exist at all because Keynes, the reformer, did not and does not exist. There is Keynes the reactionary, who hides behind reformist phraseology. There exists only

47. Volodin, *Keins—ideolog*, p. 31.   48. *Ibid.*, p. 34.

one Keynesianism, which expresses the ideology of monopolistic capital in the era of the general crisis of capitalism.[49]

Volodin maintained that Keynesianism was being used by reactionary circles, especially in the United States. Keynesian theory served as a convenient ideological cover for the imperialist ruling circles, who dreamed of conquering the world and of enslaving all its inhabitants. Keynes was alleged to be the worst enemy of peace, democracy, and socialism. Therefore, in concluding his first chapter, Volodin stressed that one of the most important tasks facing Marxist-Leninist theory was to unmask Keynesian apologetics decisively.

Volodin began his second chapter, entitled "The 'Explanation' by Keynes of the Reasons for Unemployment and Economic Crises," with appropriate quotations from Marx, Lenin, and Stalin, who had "proved" that crises and unemployment were inherent in the capitalist system. He reproduced a series of unemployment figures for the United States to demonstrate that the problem had not been solved. However, he chose years that made his case easier to prove, namely 1930 through 1938. He then returned to Keynes, whose thesis was that unemployment was caused by insufficient demand:

In fact all the stupid assertions of Keynes that comprise his "general theory of employment" come to this conclusion:
a. Unemployment arises as a result of insufficient demand.
b. Insufficient demand and consequently unemployment can be eliminated in capitalism if the state would take upon itself the function of regulating general demand.[50]

Volodin maintained that these reasons for the lack of demand were superficial. The insufficiency of demand was a consequence of the internal laws of capitalism. He was particularly severe on Keynes's psychological law to explain the lack of demand:

The absurdity and apologetic essence of this "law" is completely obvious as soon as Keynes concludes that the insufficiency of demand does not result from antagonistic capitalistic production relations but from the "nature" of man. However, this does not prevent Keynes from producing the "psychological law" that he invented as one of the basic principles of the "general theory of employment."[51]

49. *Ibid.*, p. 36.
50. *Ibid.*, p. 48.   51. *Ibid.*, p. 51.

Volodin accused Keynes of not distinguishing between classes when speaking of demand. Volodin contended that the workers had no difficulty in getting rid of extra income because they simply were not receiving any additional income. He was certain that Keynes had relied on his psychological law to cover up the problem of distribution among classes and was quick to point out the absence of this problem in the Soviet Union.

He was dissatisfied with Keynes's explanation for the lack of investment. Keynes had absolutely distorted the category of interest and thus completely confused the problem of investment:

The movement of loan capital gives rise to a series of false notions. Superficially it would seem that the part of profit that is in the form of interest falls to the money capitalist and is the fruit of capital itself, the fruit of capital as a thing. On the other hand, the part of profit that is in the form of entrepreneurial income falls to the industrial capitalist and appears in opposition to interest, as a payment for his labor. . . .[52]

As a result of the above, Keynes had removed interest from profit, of which interest was a part. Keynes had thus been able to show the false relationship between the rate of interest and the rate of profit. Volodin contended that the rate of interest did not limit investment but that interest depended on profit. He disagreed with Keynes, who had envisaged a decrease in investment when the marginal efficiency of capital was less than the rate of interest. Volodin claimed this assertion was contrary to the facts:

In reality the amount of capital investment and, consequently, the amount of production does not depend on the relationship between profit and interest, but on the existing level of profit. If the rate of profit is high and has a tendency to increase, capital investment grows and the demand of the capitalists for the means of production and labor will increase . . . .[53]

The reason Keynes had given for economic crises, Volodin continued, was that the marginal efficiency of capital fluctuated. He maintained that this theory to explain economic crises was false and that it had this quality in common with all the other bourgeois theories. He noted that the marginal efficiency of capital differed essentially in two ways from the rate of profit. First, by introducing

52. *Ibid.*, p. 55.   53. *Ibid.*, p. 58.

this concept, Keynes had disregarded the level of income that a given amount of capital will bring under existing conditions. Volodin maintained that Keynes had been able to introduce psychology into the analysis as soon as future expectations of businessmen were mentioned. Second, Keynes, by resorting to marginal analysis, had taken a subjective approach that disregarded the social content of political economy.

Volodin reduced Keynes's fluctuations in the marginal efficiency of capital to psychological expectations and the quantity of capital investments. Since these two factors supposedly work on each other, Volodin thought Keynes's theory could be called a psychological theory. He discussed optimism and pessimism and saw the reason why Keynes had emphasized them. It was simply to have the state intervene and support the optimism of the monopolist. As for Keynes's theory of crises:

> In fact the Keynesian "theory of crises" and his "theory of employment," if one can liberate them from their wordy trimmings, result in the assertion of two basic conclusions: (1) crises and unemployment produce a lowering of capitalist profits; (2) . . . an increase in the profits of the monopolists is the only means of fighting with crises and unemployment.[54]

On this subject Volodin's position was fully supported by the second edition of Academician Trakhtenberg's book on economic crises, which dealt with Keynes's theory of unemployment and crises in a similar manner: "In accordance with Keynes's theory, the reason for unemployment is the lack of demand for goods in relation to their supply. The insufficiency of this demand is the result of the psychology of the people who do not spend all their income."[55]

Trakhtenberg discussed the state as being at the service of the monopolist in Keynesian theory. However, he was more severe with Keynes in this second, revised edition than in his first. Here he did not bother to explain the Keynesian concepts as he had in his earlier edition. Instead, the class nature of Keynes's theory was given priority:

54. *Ibid.*, p. 65.
55. I. A. Trakhtenberg, *Kapitalisticheskoe vosproizvodstvo i ekonomicheskie krizisy*, 2nd ed.; (Moskva, 1954), p. 186. The first edition was discussed in chap. iii.

It is not necessary to deal with the theory of Keynes in greater detail. With the given short summary of some of the basic foundations of the theory of Keynes, it is completely sufficient to lay bare the class content of it and to understand that this theory is dispatched for the defense of the capitalist monopolies, which are not interested in the eradication of unemployment and crises but only strive for the receipt of maximum profits.[56]

Another aspect of Keynes's theory dealt with by Volodin was the role of the state in the economy, always a thorny problem for Soviet economists. To this Volodin devoted his third chapter, entitled "The Myth of the Ability of the Bourgeois State to Regulate the Economy." To understand his position on this subject, it must be noted that this question had already been thrashed out by Soviet economists prior to the publication of Volodin's book.

Academician Varga had previously been taken to task by his fellow economists precisely on this controversial issue of the role of the state in the capitalist economy. In his book *The Changes in the Economy of Capitalism as a Result of the Second World War*, Varga had assigned an important role to the state in the bourgeois economy during the war: "To put it briefly, *the bourgeois state as an organization of all the bourgeoisie was forced to try to subordinate the private interests of various enterprises and various persons to the interests of conducting the war.*"[57] Further, Varga had seen an increased role for the state in the postwar period: "With the end of the war the economic role of the state will decrease; however, it will remain significantly greater than it was prior to the war."[58]

Even though he had predicted increasing improverishment for the workers, his conclusions regarding the role of the state were unacceptable. Varga and the Institute of World Economy and World Politics, which he headed, were subjected to serious criticism. M. Myznikov, for example, in an article entitled "The Distortion of Marxism-Leninism in the Works of Academician Varga," wrote: "The views of Academician Varga present an attempt to revive the bourgeois reformist theory of 'planned,' 'organized' capitalism adapted to new circumstances which arose in the Second World

56. *Ibid.*, p. 188.
57. E. Varga, *Izmeneniya v ekonomike kapitalizma v itoge vtoroi mirovoi voiny* (Moskva, 1946), p. 18. Italics in the original.
58. *Ibid.*, p. 32.

War and the period following it."[59] Varga and his institute were further criticized by L. Gatovskii in an article entitled "Imprisoned by Bourgeois Methodology" in *Bolshevik*: "Recently the Institute of World Economy and World Politics of the Academy of Sciences of the USSR published a series of un-Marxist books about the contemporary capitalist economy."[60]

After bitter criticism, Gatovskii gave the following rule for works on capitalism:

The works of Soviet economists on the questions of the economy of the capitalist countries must be penetrated thoroughly with the spirit of bolshevik partisanship and must uncover all the contradictions of contemporary rotting, dying capitalism and serve as a fighting and attacking weapon in the battle against bourgeois ideology.[61]

Varga had mentioned Keynes in his book on two occasions. He discussed Keynes's *How to Pay for the War* to show the unifying tendency in a war economy.[62] In the second instance, he discussed Keynes's role in the international monetary conference at Bretton Woods and gave two references in the Soviet literature concerning Keynes's role in promoting international monetary stability.[63] Elsewhere in his work, he noted the planning attempts of organizations like the National Planning Association and the role of its members like Hansen, but did not mention their Keynesian influence. He thought their work would increase in the years ahead, but did not predict any success for their recommended policies.[64]

In May, 1947, Varga's book was subjected to the criticism of the academic community in a meeting officially convened for this discussion. At the first session the first speaker, M. N. Smit, in a long address found Varga weak when dealing with the bourgeoisie's plans to combat unemployment. She called these plans Keynesian:

The economists invented a series of new "theories" for the salvation of capitalism from crises. I do not have the time to discuss them but can only say that all of them are based on the notorious work of Keynes, *The*

---

59. M. Myznikov, "Izvrashcheniya Marksizma-Leninizma v rabotakh akademika E. Varga," *Planovoe Khozyaistvo*, 1948, No. 6, p. 88.

60. L. Gatovskii, "V plenu burzhuaznoi metodologii," *Bolshevik*, 1948, No. 5, p. 74.

61. *Ibid.*, p. 80.

62. Varga, *Izmeneniya v ekonomike kapitalizma*, pp. 70–71.

63. *Ibid.*, pp. 245–248.   64. *Ibid.*, p. 50.

General Theory of Employment, Money and Interest [*sic*], and they all attest to the artificial stimulation of capital investments, to the necessity of increasing consumer expenditures, and so on.[65]

In the second session of the discussion, P. A. Khromov maintained that Varga had failed to treat the problem of reparations adequately. Khromov mentioned Keynes's *The Economic Consequences of the Peace* as an example to follow, with the proviso that Varga should represent the Soviet interests as strongly as Keynes had represented the English interests.[66] Other speakers also found Varga's views to be incorrect. Kuzminov put the matter very aptly for the Soviets:

An incorrect, mistaken understanding of the role of the bourgeois state sometimes even penetrates the pages of our press. We point to the position of the Academician Varga, who reviewed the question of the war economy of the capitalist countries and propounds the un-Marxist theme that it was not the monopolies but the capitalist state in wartime that played a deciding role in the economy and that the bourgeois state can somehow introduce the principles of planning in the capitalist economy.[67]

The results of the Varga affair were that his institute was downgraded and merged with the Institute of Economics. The Varga debate shows the hostility of the Soviet policy makers to any admission of the beneficial role of the state in the capitalist system. The official role assigned to the state in the capitalist system was one of assisting the monopolies to extract maximum profits. Economic planning was not considered even a possibility in capitalism. In fact, in a letter to the editor of *Voprosy Ekonomiki*, Comrade Degtyar from Kharkov wrote for clarification on planning. He asked whether it were possible to plan in a single capitalist industry. He was disturbed on this issue as a group of his comrades, while "correctly understanding the impossibility of capitalist planning as a whole, attempt to prove the possibility of planning in a separate capitalist enterprise."[68]

65. "Diskussiya po knige E. Varga," *Mirovoe Khozyaistvo i Mirovaya Politika*, 1947, No. 11, p. 8.

66. *Ibid.*, p. 36.

67. I. Kuzminov, "O gosudarstvenno-monopolisticheskom kapitalizme," *Bolshevik*, 1948, No. 5, p. 65.

68. L. Berri, "O 'planirovanii' na kapitalisticheskom predpriyatii," *Voprosy Ekonomiki*, 1949, No. 8, p. 79.

L. Berri replied for the editor in an uncompromising tone: "Only the general state economic plan can be the basis of the planning work of each separate industry. The enterprise by itself cannot establish a plan. In conditions of anarchy in capitalist production it is impossible either to plan for the national economy as a whole or to plan the work for separate enterprises."[69]

As a result of the above discussions, the role of the state and the question of planning were settled for Volodin. In fact, according to him, this entire issue, which had once been actively debated, had now been reduced to the category of a myth:

In the general crisis of capitalism it is characteristic for bourgeois political economy to conceal its anti-people content and to propagandize widely the myth that somehow the bourgeois state is able to regulate the economic life in the direction of eliminating the anarchy of capitalist production and of liquidating economic crises, unemployment, and so forth.

Keynes is the active propagandist of this myth. The entire aggregation of the measures that he proposed for the so-called "improvement" of capitalism are in themselves, as we have already demonstrated, the justification of widespread use of the bourgeois state by monopoly capital.[70]

Volodin went on to say that Keynes had used this device as a smoke screen to deceive the workers. He quoted Stalin to the effect that the capitalist economy was not in the hands of the state but that the state was in the hands of the monopoly capitalists. Likewise, he continued that as long as capitalists and the principle of private property existed, there could be no planned economy. Like Kuzminov before him, he mentioned the sale of government enterprises to private interests in the United States following World War II. These were concrete examples of state intervention. On this basis Volodin said: "Any 'interference' by the contemporary bourgeois state in the economy, no matter how it is concealed outwardly, bears results favorable to monopoly capital. This is produced by the very class content of the contemporary bourgeois state that is at the service of the monopolies."[71] He went on to list the various forms of

69. *Ibid.*, p. 80.
70. Volodin, *Keins—ideolog*, p. 66.   71. *Ibid.*, p. 69.

state regulation that were beneficial to the monopolists—subsidies, credits, privileges, guarantees, war orders, wage reductions, and anti-worker legislation. He regarded all these examples as anti-people and reactionary.

The only distinction that Volodin saw between a peacetime and a wartime intervention in the capitalist economy was that monopolists gained more profits during wartime. Hence the war hysteria, the Marshall Plan, and the vast military preparations of the postwar period. Volodin quoted from Malenkov's report to the Nineteenth Party Congress that all the above acts would lead to war and the destruction of the capitalist system. The bourgeois state was not the common will of the entire people, Volodin asserted, and consequently it could not be above the class struggle or impartial. He was emphatic on this point and concluded his third chapter on this issue:

It is known that the bourgeois state cannot be a force above classes. It is a weapon of the class rule of the bourgeoisie, and in the period of monopoly capitalism it becomes the weapon of the financial oligarchy and is widely used for the oppression of the workers, the strengthening of the rule of the monopolies, and their enrichment at the expense of the people.[72]

Volodin's exposition of the role of the state in capitalism was the clearest statement of the prevailing official opinion. A. Kornienko echoed essentially the same analysis in an article entitled "The Reactionary Essence of the Theory of the 'Regulated Economy' of Capitalism."[73] Kornienko said the majority of bourgeois economists were propounding the theory of the regulated economy. This amounted to an apology for contemporary state-monopoly capitalism. Keynesianism was the apology of state-monopoly capitalism:

J. M. Keynes became the chief specialist in the area of adapting the reactionary ideas of the "regulation" of the economy of capitalism to the new demands of the monopolists . . . .

Keynes proclaimed the interference by the bourgeois state in the economic life as "planning" in the capitalist economy. "Planning" became in this manner the prerogative of the bourgeois state.[74]

72. *Ibid.*, p. 73.
73. A. Kornienko, "Reaktsionnaya sushchnost teorii 'reguliruemoi ekonomiki' kapitalizma," *Voprosy Ekonomiki*, 1954, No. 9, pp. 106–118.
74. *Ibid.*, pp. 109–110.

Another writer who dealt with the problem of planned capitalism was L. Alter, who devoted an entire section of *The Downfall of the Theories of "Planned Capitalism"*[75] to Keynesianism as an economic program for regulating capitalism. In this respect Keynes and *The General Theory* were given special attention, since no other bourgeois economist was given such extended treatment. Alter's book falls into two main parts. The first dealt with bourgeois theory and concluded with the section on Keynes. The second reviewed chronologically from the year 1929 the practical attempts in the West to apply the bourgeois theory of planned or regulated capitalism. All these attempts, concluded Alter, had resulted in failure.

At the present, Alter found, Keynesianism was both fashionable and current in the West. It provided the basis for the postwar policies of the United States and England:

The "theoretical" basis of the contemporary programs of "regulated capitalism" is Keynesianism—a system of bourgeois-apologetic views originated by the English bourgeois economist J. M. Keynes and his followers. Keynesianism is the main economic theory of the imperialist bourgeoisie in the period of the general crisis of capitalism . . . and the basic course for the reactionary policy of the contemporary imperialist states.[76]

Alter reviewed Keynes's life briefly and then proceeded to discuss the main proposals found in *The General Theory* to combat unemployment and economic depressions. He declared that Keynes's proposals were reactionary but packaged in democratic terms in an attempt to "eternalize" capitalism. He concluded that the entire Keynesian program was a fraud:

All the attempts to depict the "regulation of capitalism" as capitalism free from crises and unemployment are a lie and a fraud. No sort of "state regulation" can eliminate those inevitable fellow travelers of capitalism; the real and only significance of this "regulation" is to help the capitalists reduce the wages of workers to the lowest limit and to guarantee maximum profits for themselves.[77]

In his lengthy final chapter entitled "The Ideological Justification of Imperialist Reaction and War—The Essence of the Keynesian

---

75. L. Alter, *Krushenie teorii "planovogo kapitalizma"* (Moskva, 1954).
76. *Ibid.*, p. 95.   77. *Ibid.*, p. 113.

Program of 'Regulated Capitalism,' " Volodin reviewed a number of Keynesian concepts to demonstrate the hostility of Keynes toward the workers and the Soviet Union. These concepts were not taken in the same order as Keynes had presented them in *The General Theory* but seemed to be selected to make the strongest possible case against Keynes.

Volodin first dealt with Keynes as a zealous defender of inflationary methods to cause a decrease in the standard of living of the workers. To support this claim, he reviewed the Keynesian measures to increase investment by regulating the rate of interest. This was done, he continued, by establishing the false dependence of investment on the marginal efficiency of capital and the rate of interest. Volodin maintained that the Keynesian analysis was false since it ignored the most important factor, the existing amount of profit, of which interest was only a part. He claimed that Keynesian measures would lead to inflation: "The lowering of the rate of interest that Keynes proposed by means of the increased issue of paper money by the state can only lead to inflation as a consequence."[78]

Volodin maintained that issues of paper money would have no effect on the rate of interest. Demand for and supply of capital depend in the first place on the quantity of profits. In Volodin's opinion, only the workers suffered from the measures proposed by Keynes. Keynes had favored the lowering of real wages, and Volodin maintained that this policy was now in effect since the state issued paper money in addition to spending on armaments as a result of the cold war. Large debts and inflation were the only consequences, and Volodin saw the workers carrying the burden with reduced real wages and higher taxes.

The misrepresentation of Keynes's views regarding his supposed advocacy of lowering real wages by means of inflation was consistently maintained by Soviet economists. On this subject, of the numerous examples only a few will be presented here since the authors were in agreement as to their findings.[79] A. Eidelnant, writing on

78. Volodin, *Keins—ideolog*, p. 76.
79. Other articles containing substantially the same conclusions were A. Shapiro, *Voprosy Ekonomiki*, 1949, No. 2, pp. 76–91; I. Trakhtenberg, "Inflyatsiya i protsess kapitalisticheskogo vosproizvodstva," *Voprosy Ekonomiki*, 1954, No. 3, pp. 86–98; E. Bregel, "Rost nalogovogo bremeni i inflyatsiya v kapitalisticheskikh stranakh," *Voprosy Ekonomiki*, 1953, No. 2, pp. 75–91.

"The Disorder of the Capitalist Money System in the Period of the General Crisis of Capitalism," put the matter this way:

Bourgeois economists—the learned servants of monopolies—always advertise the superiority of inflation as a means of the encroachment of capital on the living standards of the working class. The vulgar "theory of wages" of the English bourgeois economist Keynes is based on the point that only the lowering of money wages will lead to strike activity and in opposition to this the gradual lowering of real wages will not produce such consequences.

Originated by Keynes and supported by many contemporary vulgar bourgeois economists, the "theory" of the different degrees of "plasticity" of money and real wages is characteristic of an epoch of chronic inflation.[80]

A. Kuznetsov was of the same opinion in his "Theory of Surplus Value—The Cornerstone of the Economic Teaching of Marx." Kuznetzov identified Keynes with the policy of lowering real wage rates: "Keynes in his book *The General Theory of Employment, Interest and Money* asserts that the increase of employment—that is, the decrease of unemployment—can occur only with the lowering of real wage rates."[81]

To return to the final chapter of Volodin's work, the author next dismissed liquidity preference as the purest nonsense. This psychological phenomenon was the cornerstone of the "notorious general theory" of the rate of interest, and Volodin said it explained nothing. He gave this account of capitalist reality:

But in true capitalist reality the level of the desire of the capitalists to hold a greater or lesser part of their capital in the form of ready money depends not on the psychological function invented by Keynes but as a whole is determined by the economic factors and in the first instance by the movement of the economic cycle.[82]

Volodin charged that Keynes had come to the defense of state monopoly capitalism under the smoke screen of the "socialization of investment." He thought Keynes had been deliberately unclear in

---

80. A. Eidelnant, "Rasstroistvo kapitalisticheskikh denezhnykh sistem v period obshchego krizisa kapitalizma," *Voprosy Ekonomiki*, 1953, No. 7, p. 38.
81. A. Kuznetsov, "Teoriya pribavochnoi stoimosti—kraeugolnyi kamen ekonomicheskogo ucheniya Marksa," *Kommunist*, 1954, No. 10, p. 100.
82. Volodin, *Keins—ideolog*, p. 80.

The General Theory as to the role the state should have in direct investment. He cited three different positions that Keynes had taken on this issue, namely, more responsibility, compromise with private initiative, and fairly widespread socialization of investment. Volodin did not leave the issue in doubt, however. He found Keynes a true supporter of state investment for the benefit of the monopolists: "By 'socialization of investment' Keynes means the nationalization of some sectors of capitalist enterprise, that is, the reorganization of private capitalist enterprises and monopolies into state-capitalist enterprises and monopolies."[83]

Volodin went on to give examples of nationalization in England. The British coal industry was losing money. Further, the industry needed modernization. Coal was a necessary raw material for other industries that would have to pay higher costs if the coal industry were to be put on a profitable basis. The solution, continued Volodin, was the single Keynesian one of socialization of investment. In this way, the former owners were fully compensated and avoided the capital loss. The state assumed the responsibility of providing coal cheaply to the other capitalist industries. The losses of the industry were passed on to the workers in the form of increased taxes. Rail transport was a similar case. The nationalization of the Bank of England was simply treated as a *de jure* recognition of a *de facto* situation. In short: "In such a manner, this so-called 'nationalization' is one of the forms of state-monopoly capitalism, namely, a form, which introduced under definite legal conditions and on a sharply limited scale, responds fully to the interests of monopoly capital."[84] And Volodin thus concluded his case against the socialization of investment:

Therefore, under capitalism the state is the weapon of the class rule of the bourgeoisie, and in the conditions of monopoly capitalism—a weapon of monopoly capital—"nationalization" of certain sectors of capitalist industry is a form of use of the state apparatus by the monopolies for its rule and the extraction of maximum profits.[85]

Volodin also found Keynes had defended monopoly capitalism under the guise of regulating private investment. He contended that

83. *Ibid.*, p. 83.
84. *Ibid.*, p. 85.   85. *Ibid.*, p. 86.

Keynes's proposals bore no resemblance to reality. The only possible regulator of capital investment was the amount of profit that was fluctuating spontaneously. The state did assist investment, he conceded, but this amounted to raiding the state treasury. The bourgeois state resorted to the militarization of the economy:

The system of war orders with their fabulously high prices and guaranteed sales of the products to the state is one of the most active forms of state "regulation" of private enterprise of the monopolies . . . .

Therefore, the basic content of state "regulation" is the enrichment of the magnates of capital at the expense of still larger robbery of the people. It cannot serve as a means of increasing general demand and forestalling of economic crises but, on the contrary, is an important factor in curtailing general demand as a result of the reduction of the effective demand of the people and leads inevitably to the further sharpening of crises.[86]

Volodin declared that the multiplier of Keynes was a false concept. The multiplier was conceived, he explained, to give a cover of pseudo-truthfulness to the state regulation of investment. Volodin defined the multiplier correctly but found it to be in scandalous contradiction to reality: reality showed that with the increase of investment the organic part of capital increased and the variable part decreased. It followed that employment would not increase as rapidly as investment and would perhaps not even increase at all. Volodin gave purported statistics for the United States for the period from 1946 through 1949. No source was given for these figures, which only showed increasing investment and increasing unemployment. The reader would not be able to tell whether over-all employment had increased during the period under review. Volodin reached a familiar conclusion on the multiplier:

In contemporary conditions of the militarization of the economy and the burdensome armaments race the fundamental purpose of the "teaching" about the "multiplier" is the justification of the huge expenditures on military preparations, in the apologetic assertions that military expenditures can somehow increase employment and lower unemployment. In reality, however, the militarization of the economy lowers the living standards of the toiling masses . . . .[87]

In a burning article entitled "Bourgeois Political Economy—

---

86. *Ibid.*, pp. 90–91.   87. *Ibid.*, p. 93.

Weapon of Warmongers," Alter had already discussed the multi-plier in similar terms but in greater detail.[88] He had distinguished between the investment multiplier and the employment multiplier, and had maintained that these concepts were at the center of Keynes's theory. He had presented more detailed statistics for ap-proximately the same period as that covered by Volodin, and he had included some data for England. In both the USA and England Alter had found investment and unemployment increasing. He, too, failed to provide any reference for his sources. Although he had dis-credited the multiplier, he had conceded its widespread use:

> However, the "theory of the multiplier" constitutes the main "theoreti-cal" foundation of the policy of the "state regulation of investment," which is followed presently by the Truman government, the Labour government, and the governments of a series of other capitalist countries. The bankrupt theory of the "multiplier" also signifies the complete insolvency of all the calculations to avert crises with the help of "state regulation" and the in-crease of investment.[89]

After discussing the multiplier Volodin turned to some of the measures that Keynes had proposed to increase personal consump-tion. His first sentence set the tone for this section: "Keynes is a zealous defender of every kind of increase of parasitical consump-tion for the exploiting classes and is a categorical enemy of any increase whatever in the impoverished consumption level of the workers."[90]

Keynes, Volodin claimed, was an open and admitted follower of Malthus' views on the possibility of overproduction and the lack of demand. He held that Keynes saw unproductive consumption as the only means to increase demand. Among the various kinds of unpro-ductive consumption, Volodin especially singled out war expendi-tures as the chief form in the capitalist system. He made reference to the profits of the capitalists and the loss of life during World War II. He completely and viciously distorted Keynes's position in regard

88. L. Alter, "Burzhuaznaya politicheskaya ekonomika—orudie podzhigatelei voiny," *Planovoe Khozyaistvo*, 1950, No. 4, pp. 63–80.
89. *Ibid.*, p. 69.
90. Volodin, *Keins—ideolog*, p. 93.

to full employment in the United States: "In 1940 in one of his journal articles, resorting to his habitual method of concealing by demagogic phraseology the aim of liquidating unemployment, Keynes openly wrote that for a country such as the USA war is the only possible means of guaranteeing 'full employment.' "[91]

Here Volodin echoes an earlier article by M. Marinin, "The Right-Wing Laborites—Servants of Anglo-American Imperialism": "The formula discovered by Keynes is exceedingly simple. He demands that the monopolists utilize the entire administrative financial system of government power to a greater degree than previously to 'regulate' investment and increase their unproductive consumption to the maximum."[92]

Volodin continued his attack by finding Keynes a zealous defender of the policy of "freezing" wages. This policy was based on the lowering of real wages through inflationary measures. Consequently this reduction appeared to be the result of the normal working of economic laws. Volodin found that Keynes had based this policy on the principle of diminishing productivity, a variation of the principle of diminishing returns on land. This principle, Volodin declared, had been discredited long ago by Marx himself. Keynes's analysis was too rigid as a result of his assumptions. He had not taken into account the constant increase in labor productivity and the colossal growth of unused productive capacity of existing plants. Overlooking these considerations, Keynes had still advocated lowering real wages to increase employment: "On the basis of the 'principle' of the diminishing marginal product of labor Keynes concludes as though the only means of increasing employment is the lowering of wages. He proclaims . . . that the increase of employment can only take place with the lowering of real wage rates."[93]

Volodin found Keynes's thinking on wages similar to the "notorious" theory of the wage fund. Keynes's contention that real and nominal wages move in opposite directions was sufficient to unmask

91. *Ibid.*, p. 95.
92. M. Marinin, "Pravye leiboristy—prisluzhniki anglo-amerikanskogo imperializma," *Bolshevik*, 1951, No. 10, p. 66.
93. Volodin, *Keins—ideolog*, pp. 96–97.

him as the chief proponent of reducing living standards of the workers by inflationary methods. Volodin concluded that *The General Theory* provided the justification of the current policy of the wage freeze in the capitalist countries:

> In this manner, Keynes's "general theory" of wages is the ideological justification of the "freezing" of nominal wages and the systematic growth of prices of goods. It is namely this method of encroachment on the living standards of the workers that serves as the basis of the policy of state "regulation" of wages and prices in capitalist countries at the present time.[94]

A section of the book is devoted to the "euthanasia of the rentier." Volodin called this idea of Keynes a fabrication and a clear example of demagoguery. Further, he did not think that the repulsive features of capitalism would be removed with euthanasia. He saw no prospect of the rate of interest falling to zero in the capitalist system. This theory concerning euthanasia had been propounded by Keynes in order to sow harmful reformist illusions. Volodin admitted that the concept was original in that it justified the increase of profits to the limit, and that the monopolists would accumulate capital to such an extent that the income from it would fall to zero. But the workers were to assist the scheme by increasing their own exploitation.

Volodin mentioned other reformist ideas regarding interest that were discredited. He singled out the fascist slogan of the freedom of "interest slavery" that deceived the working classes of Germany when Hitler came to power. Keynes's euthanasia of the rentier, Volodin maintained, was of the same demagogic character. Capitalism and its attendant evils could not be cured by this method:

> It is completely obvious that as long as capitalism exists, interest, which is a part of profit, will also exist, and also the rentier—this most parasitical member of the capitalist class . . . . To conceal the irreconcilable class contradictions between the working class and the bourgeoisie and to divert the proletariat from the revolutionary struggle against the rotting capitalist system—those are the aims that Keynes seeks when he calls on the trite, apologetic thesis of the possibility of liquidating interest in capitalism.[95]

In the concluding section of his last chapter, Volodin found that Keynes's apologetic theory was widely accepted by contemporary

94. *Ibid.*, p. 99.   95. *Ibid.*, p. 102.

bourgeois economists. Although varieties of Keynesian theories had appeared, Volodin maintained that there was very little difference among them:

All of them are based on one and the same vulgar position and seek the single and same goal—the apology for contemporary capitalism and the defense of the interests of monopoly capital. They all proceed from the basis that the reason for the "defects" of contemporary capitalism is found in the insufficiency of demand, and the possibility of liquidating these defects—in the regulation of demand by the state.[96]

In a review of the proposals of the Keynesians in the United States and England, Beveridge, Hansen, Chase, Lorwin, and Harris were mentioned. Volodin insisted that the main content of their Keynesianism was the justification of imperialist wars and reaction at the expense of the workers. In his final paragraph he again concluded with the customary prediction that this policy would fail:

The attempts of the ruling classes and their "learned" servants to find prescriptions to cure capitalism, which has outlived its age by means of further encroachment on the living standards of the people, the establishment of fascist regimes, and the unleashing of wars, will have their own inevitable consequence in the hastening final destruction of capitalism.[97]

The thesis that militarization was a basic tenet of Keynes and his followers was constantly found in the literature of the period. Blyumin's "Bourgeois Economists in the Service of Militarism and War" identified Keynes and his followers with militarization: "Keynes and his followers consciously obliterate the difference between productive and unproductive expenditures of capital in order to inculcate in the reader the idea that the influence of militarization is somehow 'beneficial' to the economy of the capitalist countries."[98]

V. Cheprakov's "Bourgeois Economists of the USA—Apologists of Imperialist Reaction and Aggression" stamped Keynesian economics as the ideological support for the armaments race: "Bourgeois economists of the Keynesian doctrine with their 'theories' of so-called compensating expenditures of the state proclaim the arma-

---

96. *Ibid.*, pp. 102–103.   97. *Ibid.*, p. 119.
98. I. Blyumin, "Burzhuaznye ekonomisty na sluzhbe militarizma i voiny," *Voprosy Ekonomiki*, 1952, No. 9, p. 115.

ments race as a wonder-working device for all the internal contradictions of capitalism and for saving it from crises."[99]

Similarly, N. Dmitriev identified Keynes with a military policy in
an article entitled "Progressive Economists of the USA in the Struggle Against the Ideology of Militarism and Reaction":

After the failure of numerous anti-crisis projects, bourgeois political
economy declared the war economy as the chief means of "curing" capitalism from the crises of overproduction. Bourgeois theoreticians discovered the "secret of prosperity" of capitalism in the militarization of the
economy, which was based on the conception of the English economist
J. M. Keynes.[100]

In the course of Volodin's book, a recurrent theme had been that
of unemployment in the bourgeois West. This theme was constantly
echoed by other Soviet economists throughout the period. Unemployment was inevitable under capitalism, and Keynes's theory was
found to be inadequate in dealing with this defect of the capitalist
system. In fact, the writers of the period found that the "law" of the
absolute and relative impoverishment of the workers was still in effect. V. Chermenskii's article entitled "The Impoverishment of the
Workers in the Capitalist Countries" had this to say of Keynes:

The growth of unemployment in the USA and other capitalist countries
signifies the complete crushing of the demagoguery concerning "full employment" under capitalism that has been fashionable in recent years. Following the English economist Keynes, who published his program for "full
employment" fifteen years ago, many English and American bourgeois
economists lost a great deal of energy in order to prove the possibility of
achieving "full employment" or an exceedingly high measure of "high employment" under capitalism . . . . But in reality unemployment is an inevitable fellow traveler of capitalism.[101]

The phrase "the inevitable fellow traveler of capitalism" was very
popular and became a well-worn cliché during the period under re-

99. V. Cheprakov, "Burzhuaznye ekonomisty SShA—apologety imperialisticheskoi reaktsii i agressii," *Bolshevik*, 1952, No. 24, p. 103.

100. N. Dmitriev, "Progressivnye ekonomisty SShA v borbe protiv ideologii militarizma i reaktsii," *Voprosy Ekonomiki*, 1955, No. 2, p. 70.

101. V. Chermenskii, "Obnishchanie trudyashchikhsya v kapitalisticheskikh stranakh," *Planovoe Khozyaistvo*, 1950, No. 2, p. 80.

view. D. I. Valentei even wrote a book on the subject of unemployment entitled *Unemployment—Inevitable Fellow Traveler of Capitalism,*[102] in which he gave a historical account of unemployment in the capitalist countries, devoting his final chapter to "demagogic" bourgeois theories of full employment:

The "theories" of regulating unemployment in the conditions of capitalism by means of state intervention in the economic life of capitalistic countries have the greatest circulation among bourgeois economists. J. Keynes, for example, considers the possibility of reducing unemployment by means of regulating consumption, investment, and the rate of interest by the state.[103]

Valentei inevitably found that the Keynesians only served the monopolists. He said that the Keynesian program used unproductive consumption as a means of reducing unemployment. This meant luxuries for the wealthy capitalists who received super-profits from state orders for military goods. This did not reduce unemployment, Valentei continued, and Keynes's theories were found to be unscientific and reactionary:

This assertion like other theoretical propositions of Keynes and the Keynesians cannot withstand serious criticism on the ways to alleviate unemployment in the capitalist countries. The prescriptions of Keynes on the alleviation of unemployment are false and demagogic. Attempting to create the appearance of objectivity in his views and striving to conceal the deepest contradictions of capitalism, Keynes stands for the preservation of super-profits, the wasteful consumption of the bourgeoisie, and the preservation of large-scale unemployment.[104]

All through this period Keynes's theories received virulent criticism from Soviet economists. An example of the bitterness of this campaign was I. Blyumin's review of Harrod's biography of Keynes in an article entitled "Keynesianism in the Service of Imperialist Reaction."[105] Blyumin declared Keynes to be an avowed anti-Marxist

---

102. D. I. Valentei, *Bezrabotitsa—neizbezhnyi sputnik kapitalizma* (Moskva, 1951).
103. *Ibid.,* p. 228.   104. *Ibid.,* pp. 230–231.
105. I. Blyumin, "Keinsianstvo na sluzhbe imperialisticheskoi reaktsii," *Voprosy Ekonomiki,* 1952, No. 2, pp. 123–126.

throughout his life: "Keynes considered his very first task to be the struggle against Marxism and the revolutionary worker's movement. Anti-Marxist and anti-Soviet attacks comprise the basic leitmotiv in all his works."[106]

After a short review of the Keynesian program, Blyumin turned his attention to Harrod's book. Harrod, he felt, had tried to exalt Keynes in every possible way. In this attempt Harrod had introduced a great many of Keynes's published articles. But in Blyumin's opinion these articles provided valuable material to show Keynes to be "a cynical intriguer, the worst enemy of the working class and the toiling masses, and the trusted servant of contemporary imperialism."[107]

Blyumin gave several examples of Keynes's anti-Marxist activities. Among these were included the letter to Shaw in which Keynes had hoped his theory would "overthrow" the foundations of Marxism. Blyumin reviewed the reasons why Marxists should combat Keynesianism. He concluded that Harrod's work would provide a useful weapon:

In the struggle against Keynesianism one can use the numerous facts introduced in Harrod's book. Despite the intentions of the author, this book by the zealous Keynesian shows once again the bankruptcy of the bourgeois legend about Keynes as the "liberal figure," "reformist" and "pacifist." Keynes was the servant of the monopolies and the worst enemy of the working class.[108]

During this period the entry on Keynes in the second edition of the *Great Soviet Encyclopedia* also underwent a striking change. In the first edition (1936) the entry on Keynes was inoffensive and substantially objective. The second edition revealed a new tone characteristic of this period:

Keynes, John Maynard (1883–1946)—English vulgar bourgeois economist, ideologist of imperialist reaction and wars, unmasked by V. I. Lenin in 1920 as an "avowed bourgeois, a ruthless opponent of bolshevism, which he, as an English philistine, pictures in an ugly, savage and brutal

106. *Ibid.*, p. 123.
107. *Ibid.*, p. 124.   108. *Ibid.*, p. 126.

manner" . . . . All the activity of Keynes, the zealous enemy of the working class and apologist of the fascist imperialist bourgeoisie, was directed to strengthening the power of the monopolies under the cover of demagogic "anti-crises" phrases . . . .[109]

Except for *The General Theory*, this article failed to mention any of Keynes's works, even those which had been translated into Russian. This entry was more than twice the length of the original article and contained a scurrilous attack on Keynes and his theory.

Such was the Soviet position on Keynes during the height of the cold war. The Russian translation of *The General Theory* had resulted in a large output of Soviet works on Keynes. It was not surprising to find these works highly critical of *The General Theory*, but the extent of this criticism and the bitterness of its tone was indicative of the length to which the Soviets went in portraying Keynes in a most unfavorable light. During this period the Soviets probably gave more criticism and attention to Keynes than to all the other Western economists taken together. Presumably the increasingly hysterical note to be found in Soviet attacks on Keynes is due to the fact that after the war the Soviets were gradually becoming aware of the possible success of Keynesianism in prolonging the life of capitalism despite their dire predictions of its imminent collapse.

The Soviet position on Keynes shifted during the cold war period. Previously, Keynes and his role were recognized, but he was not identified as *the* ideologist of monopoly capitalism. He shared criticism with others of the West. Now he was given this special role, and his theory was held to be responsible for Western economic policy during this period, including the Marshall Plan and other policies of the United States and British governments. Even the Soviet general reference works reflected this change in emphasis. Keynes, in the opinion of the Soviets, was now designated as the chief ideologist of the imperialist West in the battle of two world economic systems, socialism and capitalism. They ascribed to Keynesian policies all the evils of the capitalist system, such as unemployment, militarization of the economy, economic crises, and so forth, and even refused to

109. *Bolshaya Sovetskaya Entsiklopediya*, 2nd ed.; XX (June, 1953), 488–489. The entry in the first edition was reviewed in chap. ii.

admit the possibility of successful state intervention in the capitalist economy. Their chief spokesman appeared to be the extremist Volodin. The level of criticism was appallingly low and repetitive. The constant use of abusive adjectives and phrases, such as "repulsive," "rotting," the "sores of the capitalist system," etc., by the Soviet writers was evidence of the poverty of their arguments. The use of these stock phrases reflected the stagnation of real critical thought and complete subservience to the official line on Keynes.

VI. *The Keynesian International*

The Soviets concentrated their criticism on Keynes himself at the height of the cold war period, while recognizing his vast influence throughout the Western world. They identified Keynes's theory as the economic basis for current reformist and revisionist movements within various socialist and social democratic parties whose ideology, in their judgment, was a revision of Marxism. These reformist policies were to improve the capitalist system and in some cases eventually transform it into socialism by peaceful means. These ideas ran counter to the official orthodox position of the Soviets, which called for a revolutionary overthrow of the capitalist system by the proletariat.

This concern on the part of the Soviets with reformism and revisionism was and is indeed a serious one. In fact, the Soviets are continuously occupied with these movements within their own sphere of influence, as well as in the world at large. The concern here is with Keynes and the role the Soviets have assigned to him in revisionist movements and in reformist policies. The Soviets began to consider the spread of Keynesianism in the West, and even found signs of it in satellite countries such as Yugoslavia and Poland. Articles and books on the subject appeared, chiefly under the auspices of the Academy of Sciences. However, even non-technical and non-economic journals, and journals published in the outlying Soviet republics, began to carry articles on the spread of Keynesianism and its influence on revisionist and reformist movements.

Among the first to recognize the influence of Keynes on government policies was Academician Trakhtenberg in an article entitled "The Transition of the Capitalist Countries from a Wartime to a Peacetime Economy."[1] Trakhtenberg discussed the various plans

1. I. Trakhtenberg, "Perekhod kapitalisticheskikh stran ot voennoi k mirnoi ekonomike," *Mirovoe Khozyaistvo i Mirovaya Politika*, 1946, Nos. 4–5, pp. 1–32.

to provide full employment in the United States and Great Britain, and found that the majority of these plans were based on the theory of Keynes.[2]

Blyumin, in his introductory article to the Russian translation of Keynes's *The General Theory* also noted that Keynesianism had become not merely a national but an international ideology:

That Keynes uses social demagoguery, that he carefully conceals the reactionary tendencies of his program, that he proclaims such popular slogans as the fight against unemployment, that he criticizes some short-comings of the capitalist system, make Keynesianism altogether suitable as an ideological weapon for the right-wing socialists. In fact, Keynesianism has become the basic economic program of the laborites, the French socialists, and of all international social democrats in general.[3]

In reviewing the policies of imperialism in the period following World War II, Academician Varga discussed the position of the right-wing social democrats in Western capitalist countries. He found that the Keynesian influence was predominant among social democrats: "Openly denying Marxism, they do not and cannot have an independent ideology that is different from that of the bourgeoisie. In the area of economics they uphold the theory of Keynes, the ideologist of the bourgeoisie."[4]

Varga's findings were echoed by Blyumin and Dvorkin in an article entitled "On the Contemporary Political Economy of the In-Between Classes."[5] The authors recalled that Marx and Engels had mentioned groups between the proletariat and the capitalist classes. It was found that Marxism-Leninism provided the political economy for the proletariat and that Keynesianism was the ideology of the capitalists. In addition, Blyumin and Dvorkin investigated the political economy of the in-between groups and contended that it was Keynesian as well: "Keynesianism—this is the most widely disseminated bourgeois theory in the period of the general crisis of capitalism . . . and is accepted by all right-wing socialist economists."[6]

2. *Ibid.*, p. 18.
3. Keins, *Teoriya*, pp. xiii–xiv.
4. E. Varga, *Osnovnye voprosy ekonomiki i politiki imperializma* (Moskva, 1953), p. 436.
5. I. Blyumin and I. Dvorkin, "O sovremennoi politicheskoi ekonomii promezhu-tochnykh klassov," *Voprosy Ekonomiki*, 1955, No. 9, pp. 148–162.
6. *Ibid.*, p. 153.

The authors concluded that Keynesianism had penetrated the thinking of the right-wing socialists and social reformers, who both fell into this middle category: "After World War II the economic theories of the right-wing social democrats became to a significant degree opportunistic shelters of Keynesianism."[7]

The history of revisionism was reviewed briefly by G. Kozlov in an article entitled "The Triumph of the Theory of Scientific Communism."[8] Kozlov outlined the dangers of revisionism, which he identified with Keynesianism:

In Keynesianism the social democrats found the theoretical "basis" of their attempts to replace the revolutionary struggle for socialism by niggardly reforms. The theory of Keynes is propagated by reformists as a doctrine that somehow provides the possibility of basic improvement in the position of the working class by means of regulating the economy by the bourgeois state.[9]

The Institute of World Economy and International Relations of the Academy of Sciences of the USSR published a collection of articles in book form entitled *Reformism, Revisionism, and Problems of Contemporary Capitalism.*[10] In an article entitled "On the Question of State Monopoly Capitalism," L. Leontev admitted that the state played a part in the economic life of every capitalist country but maintained that this part was detrimental to the workers. Keynesianism, in his opinion, was the economic theory that justified the role of the state in the economy:

Keynesianism is the chief school of bourgeois apologetics in the area of political economy in present conditions. It is namely this theory of Keynes and his followers that, in the estimate of the bourgeoisie, is called upon to oppose Marxism successfully in the period of the general crisis of capitalism.[11]

Leontev was certain that any opposition to Marxism would end in dismal failure. His analysis of Keynesianism was simple and brief:

---

7. *Ibid.,* p. 154.
8. G. Kozlov, "Torzhestvo teorii nauchnogo kommunizma," *Voprosy Ekonomiki,* 1958, No. 5, pp. 9–19.
9. *Ibid.,* p. 14.
10. Akademiya Nauk SSSR, *Reformizm, revizionizm i problemy sovremennogo kapitalizma* (Moskva, 1959).
11. *Ibid.,* p. 32.

The alpha and omega of Keynesianism is to whitewash state monopoly capitalism in every way. The Keynesians portray this as a system in which all the good sides of capitalism are preserved but the bad sides are eliminated. Contemporary reformists and revisionists praise in unison these Keynesian revelations and attribute to them the quality of the last word of science. They proclaim as "regulation of the economy" and "planning" all those measures by the bourgeois state that increase the power of the monopolies and guarantee their receiving gigantic super-profits.[12]

In addition to identifying Keynesianism with revisionist and reformist groups, the Soviets held Keynesianism responsible for the economic policies of the major capitalist countries following World War II. The Soviets gave special attention and emphasis to the policies of the United States and Great Britain, the leading capitalist powers after the war. In the battle between the two systems, socialist and capitalist, they received the brunt of Soviet criticism, being treated both separately and together in the numerous works written by Soviets during this postwar period.

A representative example of this criticism was an article entitled "The Bourgeois 'Theories' of National Income in the Service of Imperialism" by F. Grachev,[13] who maintained that the constantly increasing war budgets of the capitalist countries meant impoverishment for the workers. Grachev found that bourgeois theories of national income distribution were used to explain these budget increases. The Keynesian theory was the current bourgeois theory, and Grachev had this to say about it:

The reactionary, militaristic theory of Keynes, which is preached by contemporary Keynesians, the American economists Boulding and Ayres, the English reactionary Beveridge, and others, is now used by the most aggressive circles of American and English monopoly capital, who are acquiring fabulous profits, for the future redistribution of the national income in their favor with the help of the bourgeois state.

The false, reactionary theory of the redistribution of national income that is based on Keynesian ideas is openly accepted by the right-wing socialists and especially the laborites in the service of Anglo-American imperialism.[14]

12. *Ibid.*, p. 33.
13. F. Grachev, "Burzhuaznye 'teorii' natsionalnogo dokhoda na sluzhbe imperializma," *Voprosy Ekonomiki*, 1953, No. 4, pp. 50–60.
14. *Ibid.*, p. 57.

In his book *The Downfall of the Theories of "Planned Capitalism,"* Alter devoted an entire section to Keynesianism as the economic program of "regulated capitalism."[15] He discussed Keynesian policies in the United States and Great Britain throughout his book and found that Keynes's influence was paramount in these countries:

It is namely this theory of "regulated capitalism" and the practical prescriptions of "economic regulation" derived from it that are widely used at the present time by the governments of the imperialist states in the policy of the militarization of the economy and the preparation of a new war. The idea of "regulated capitalism" contained in its nature the "theoretical" basis for the economic policy of the Truman government; the present Eisenhower government stems from it; and the Conservative government in England and the governments of other bourgeois states adhere to it.[16]

M. N. Ryndina's book *Bourgeois Economists of England and the USA in the Service of Imperialist Reaction*[17] dealt with the Keynesian influence in those countries. Ryndina also found that Keynesianism was the ideology of monopoly capitalism and that it was disseminated widely after World War II. The first chapter on Keynesianism, the longest in the book, was divided into two parts, the second of which was entitled "The Dissemination of Keynesianism in England and the USA after the Second World War."

Ryndina reviewed the 1945 Labour Government's program of nationalization and rejected it as "typical bourgeois nationalization." She discussed the Beveridge plan and the works of several English and American Keynesians. "In attempting to justify the policies of the magnates of monopoly capital, the American Keynesians in a significant measure more than Keynes himself praise the bourgeois state while skimming over its classical position and function."[18] The American Keynesians, in Ryndina's opinion, attempted to justify the aggressive foreign policy of the United States. They supported the Marshall Plan and even called for war: "The American Keynesians openly appear as warmongers calling for a new war and propagate cosmopolitanism."[19]

---

15. Alter, *Krushenie teorii "planovogo kapitalizma,"* pp. 94–114.
16. *Ibid.*, p. 94.
17. M. N. Ryndina, *Burzhuaznye ekonomisty Anglii i SShA na sluzhbe imperialisticheskoi reaktsii* (Moskva, 1954).
18. *Ibid.*, p. 60.   19. *Ibid.*, p. 73.

The foregoing paragraphs analyzed only a representative selection from the many works available on Keynesian economic theory as the basis for economic policy in the United States and Great Britain.[20] These two countries also received individual attention from the Soviets. In particular, the Labour party's rise to power following World War II led to much adverse criticism from the Soviets, since its policies were found to be reformist and strongly influenced by Keynesianism.

L. Ya. Eventov of the Institute of World Economy and World Politics in *The War Economy of England*[21] discussed the postwar prospects of England as well as its performance during the war. In his opinion, unemployment would be the main problem facing postwar England. He mentioned two English projects designed to combat unemployment in peacetime, a study by Lever Brothers and Unilever Ltd. entitled *The Problem of Unemployment* and the book *Full Employment in a Free Society*, by William Beveridge. Eventov contended that both these plans were based on Keynesian thinking. He explained simply and briefly the general concepts of *The General Theory* as a background to these plans, then discussed the Beveridge plan at greater length and was reasonably objective in his description of it. Eventov's criticism was relatively mild; he thought the plan too utopian.[22]

At this time the Labour party was in power and was subjected to heavy criticism by Dvorkin in his article "Laborism—the Ideological Support of Imperialism."[23] Dvorkin condemned the activities of Douglas Jay, Hugh Dalton, Stafford Cripps, Herbert Morrison, and Clement Attlee as reactionary and anti-worker. These men, he contended, were following Keynesian policies:

> The bourgeois nature of the bosses of the Labour party in its active and truly anti-worker policy is especially and sharply revealed. Accepting the

20. Other relevant works on this subject were D. I. Valentei, *Bezrabotitsa—neizbezhnyi sputnik kapitalizma* (Moskva, 1951); I. G. Blyumin, *O sovremennoi burzhuaznoi politicheskoi ekonomii* (Moskva, 1958); N. N. Lyubimov, *Mezhdunarodnyi kapitalisticheskii kredit—orudie imperialisticheskoi agressii* (Moskva, 1951).

21. L. Ya. Eventov, *Voennaya ekonomika Anglii* (Moskva, 1946).

22. *Ibid.*, pp. 270–271.

23. I. Dvorkin, "Leiborizm—ideinaya opora imperializma," *Voprosy Ekonomiki*, 1949, No. 5, pp. 61–82. For an earlier but essentially similar article see Lemin, *Bolshevik*, 1948, No. 6, pp. 43–61.

economic views of Keynes, the ideologist of monopoly capital, the right-wing laborites put into practice his reactionary postulates of not allowing the increase of nominal wages of workers despite the price increases of consumer goods.[24]

Dvorkin maintained his interest in this area as he returned to the attack in 1953 with a full-length work entitled *The Ideology and Politics of the Right-wing Laborites in the Service of Monopolies.*[25] In this book he reviewed the entire history of the right-wing laborites in England. He was still of the opinion that Keynesianism was the present ideology of the Labour party: "The reactionary bourgeois economist John Maynard Keynes became the real idol of the right-wing laborites before and after the Second World War. His book *The General Theory of Employment, Interest and Money* was received by the labor bosses with joy."[26]

Dvorkin devoted a chapter to showing the connection between the policies of the Labour party and Keynesian theory. According to him, the labor bosses saw in Keynes the fulfilment of their own policies of demagoguery to deceive the workers and thereby strengthen capitalism. Dvorkin provided quotes from various laborites to show their indebtedness to Keynes's influence. However, he contended that Keynes had borrowed the major tenets of his theory from a variety of sources. In this respect Dvorkin found Keynes to be an eclectic following his teacher, Alfred Marshall.

The principal concepts of Keynes's theory were reviewed and rejected. The standard Soviet arguments were provided by Dvorkin. For example, to increase profits it was necessary to increase demand for luxury goods:

> In order to increase demand for goods and thereby guarantee the increase of profits, Keynes proposes to increase significantly the consumption of the bourgeoisie, welcoming the most senseless luxury and the most absurd expenses of the bourgeoisie—even up to the construction of luxurious tombs and so forth.[27]

Dvorkin castigated the policy of lowering real wages through inflationary methods. This policy resulted in higher taxes for the work-

---

24. Dvorkin, *Voprosy Ekonomiki*, 1949, No. 5, pp. 72–73.
25. I. Dvorkin, *Ideologiya politiki pravykh leiboristov na sluzhbe monopolii* (Moskva, 1953).
26. *Ibid.*, p. 239.   27. *Ibid.*, p. 244.

ers but gigantic subsidies to the capitalists. The theory and practice of the Keynesians benefited only the capitalists. The capitalists welcomed Keynes's theory, and it was also the theory of the right-wing laborites, who were in the service of the monopolists. Dvorkin noticed that the laborites did not popularize this fact. Instead, they fastened their own labels of the "leveling of income" and "socialism" onto Keynesian policies.

It goes without saying that the right-wing laborites up to the time they took office could not announce in their program an open and direct statement of the Keynesian theory of lowering real wages and increasing the profits of capitalists. Even Keynes himself veiled these demands with the chatter about the "euthanasia of the rentier."[28]

The Labour party preferred, Dvorkin continued, to speak about the regulation of investment and full employment that was supposed to benefit the people and increase their living standards. Dvorkin concentrated on the regulation of investment by the state and avoided the issue of full employment. Perhaps this was due to the fact that England was experiencing full employment during this period. In any event, he gave several examples where the state provided investments, subsidies, and orders to various industries. In his analysis, all these funds were channeled into the pockets of the capitalists in the way of profits. This was the essence, he concluded, of the Labour party's program:

If we were to put it all into simple language, then the following would result. The Labour Government, which is acting according to Keynes, reduces the consumption of the workers. Through subsidization it directs to private capital the basic mass of funds which the Labour Government allocates to capital investment. Capital investment, not considering direct war appropriations, goes primarily *to the preparation of war*.[29]

Professor Blyumin's *A Critique of the Contemporary Bourgeois Political Economy of England*[30] appeared at the same time as Dvorkin's work mentioned above. Blyumin reviewed the evolution of

28. *Ibid.*, p. 249.

29. *Ibid.*, p. 255. Similar conclusions were found in the following sources: M. Marinin, "Pravye sotsialisty prisluzhniki imperialistov," *Bolshevik*, 1952, No. 7, pp. 73–80; S. Vygodskii, "Osnovnoi ekonomicheskii zakon sovremennogo kapitalizma," *Kommunist*, 1952, No. 22, pp. 35–52; Volodin, *Keins—ideolog*, pp. 86–89.

30. I. G. Blyumin, *Kritika sovremennoi burzhuaznoi politicheskoi ekonomii Anglii* (Moskva, 1953).

bourgeois political economy in the context of the general crisis of capitalism and the battle of the two systems. His conclusions were that political economy in England was an apology for state-monopoly capitalism and a justification for the oppression of the working class. Keynesianism was given priority throughout his analysis, since Blyumin found it to be the predominant theory for the justification of capitalism in England: "Keynesianism is the ruling trend in contemporary English bourgeois economic literature."[31]

Blyumin maintained that the right-wing laborites were the propagandists for bourgeois political economy. Here he referred to Christopher Mayhew, Clement Attlee, A. L. Rowse, Hugh Dalton, Herbert Morrison, John Strachey, R. H. Crossman, Douglas Jay, G. D. H. Cole, and others as persons who leaned heavily on Keynesian theory.[32] Laborites, continued Blyumin, hated communism more than anyone else, and they resolutely opposed Marxism. They diverted the workers from the class struggle, and they resorted to Keynesianism to accomplish this end. Blyumin agreed with Dvorkin that the laborites peddled Keynesianism in disguise:

Taking the role of propagandists of the reactionary "theories" of vulgar political economy, the laborites mask these "theories," Keynesianism in particular, with socialist phraseology. They have completely distorted the essence of socialism, proclaiming it to be a special variety of capitalism in order to make the most use of the reactionary views of Keynes and his followers.[33]

The fact, concluded Blyumin, that the right-wing labor leadership had seized upon Keynesianism as their ideological armament was proof of the deep decay of their present status. After a lengthy review of the policies of the Labour party during its term of office, Blyumin declared it to be anti-worker and anti-Soviet. Further, the laborites were nothing more than the left-wing of the conservatives in England.

From the foregoing, it can be seen how heavily the British social-

31. *Ibid.*, p. 97.   33. Blyumin, *Kritika*, p. 104.
32. *Ibid.*, pp. 75–113. Other articles referring to leading personalities in the English labor movement in connection with Keynesianism: E. Bregel, "Burzhuaznye i revizionistskie teorii 'smeshannoi ekonomiki,'" *Voprosy Ekonomiki*, 1958, No. 8, pp. 66–80; P. Oldak, "Keinsianstvo—teoreticheskaya osnova sovremennogo opportunizma," *Mirovaya Ekonomika i Mezhdunarodnye Otnosheniya*, 1958, No. 12, pp. 129–131.

ists were condemned by the Soviets for adapting their policies to the theories of Keynes, which, the Soviets declared, were at the basis of nationalization, falling wages, rising profits, unproductive expenditures, and militarization. This is in striking contrast to an earlier Soviet opinion of the Labour party by I. Lemin, who wrote that the victory of the Labour party in 1945 was a historical landmark in English political life: "The result of this election in England is a witness to the great progress that has come about in the social life and consciousness of the people as the result of the victorious war against Hitlerite Germany."[34]

The Soviets also published many works specifically devoted to American economic policy, largely in the form of articles that condemned American policies as imperialist and accused the economists propounding these policies as servants or lackeys of imperialism. A typical example is D. Shepilov's article entitled "The Swordbearers of American Imperialism."[35] Shepilov had in mind the contributors to *Saving American Capitalism* (New York, 1948), edited by Seymour E. Harris. The thinking behind this work, Shepilov found, was Keynesian:

> The learned servants [the bourgeois economists] warned their masters that American capitalism will not survive if "surgery" is not quickly performed. However, the measures offered to save American capitalism are not brilliantly new or original . . . . These are the very same apologetic ideas of Keynes on the system of state-monopoly capitalism . . . .[36]

That the influence of Keynes was not to be underestimated during this period was the point made by A. Shapiro in his article "The Marshall Plan, the Violence of Militarism, and the Economic Crisis in the USA."[37] Keynesianism, Shapiro maintained, was the basis for

34. I. Lemin, "Pobeda leiboristskoi partii na parlamentskikh vyborakh v Anglii," *Bolshevik*, 1945, No. 15, p. 63.

35. D. Shepilov, "Oruzhenostsy amerikanskogo imperializma," *Bolshevik*, 1949, No. 18, pp. 54–72. Other articles on this theme: I. Trakhtenberg, "Antinauchnye domysly uchennykh lakeev monopolisticheskogo kapitala," *Bolshevik*, 1952, No. 15, pp. 74–80; V. Cheprakov, "Burzhuaznye ekonomisty SShA—apologety imperialisticheskoi reaktsii i agressii," *Bolshevik*, 1952, No. 24, pp. 93–107; V. Cheprakov, "Burzhuaznye ekonomisty i gosudarstvenno-monopolisticheskii kapitalizm," *Voprosy Ekonomiki*, 1955, No. 9, pp. 134–147.

36. Shepilov, *Bolshevik*, 1949, No. 18, p. 59.

37. A. Shapiro, "Plan Marshalla, razgul militarizma i ekonomicheskii krizis v SShA," *Voprosy Ekonomiki*, 1950, No. 8, pp. 125–131.

the Truman policy of regulating the economy. Shapiro referred to William Z. Foster, the head of the American Communist party, for support in taking Ya. A. Kronrod to task for downgrading Keynesianism:

This is why W. Foster especially underlines the necessity of unmasking Keynesianism as the basis of the contemporary ideology of state-monopoly capitalism. Ya. A. Kronrod in his review of the collection of articles entitled "Economic Crisis and the Cold War" criticizes its authors for the "well-known overvaluation of the significance of the figure of Keynes and the notorious Keynesian doctrine." This "over-valuation" was imagined by Comrade Kronrod; and on the contrary, it follows that we should welcome in every way possible the criticism by Comrade Foster of the reactionary Keynesian ideology.[38]

Blyumin, the Soviet authority on bourgeois economic thought, wrote another full-length work entitled *An Outline of Contemporary Bourgeois Political Economy in the USA*.[39] Blyumin's book was the first to appear in the postwar period that dealt with political economy in America. It reviewed bourgeois political economy from colonial times through the period following World War II. In dealing with the period of imperialism and the general crisis of capitalism, Blyumin designated two schools for special attention. The first was Institutionalism, which gave way to the second school, Keynesianism, during the depression. Institutionalism had failed, Blyumin explained, because it had failed to develop new forms of apologetics and to influence the masses.[40] Keynesianism was better suited to deceive the masses and won the day. Blyumin contended that many Institutionalists even crossed lines and became Keynesians: "Keynesianism became the most suitable ideological weapon of contemporary capitalism, and in this respect the American as well."[41]

Blyumin's treatment of Keynesianism was fairly extensive, and the most prominent American Keynesians were mentioned (these included Alvin Hansen, Seymour E. Harris, Lawrence R. Klein, and K. K. Kurihari) and reference was made to their works. Blyumin

38. *Ibid.*, p. 131. The reference to Kronrod's review was *Sovetskaya Kniga*, 1950, No. 7, p. 87.
39. Blyumin, *Ocherki sovremennoi burzhuaznoi politicheskoi ekonomii SShA.*
40. *Ibid.*, p. 67.   41. *Ibid.*, p. 69.

128

emphasized the widespread dissemination that Keynesian ideas had received in American economic literature. Two of the ideas singled out for attention were the campaigns against the gold standard and the balanced budget. Blyumin's review noticed the existence of other schools on the American scene: "Keynesianism is the most typical school of bourgeois political economy in the USA. Along with the Keynesian theory in American economic literature there are many other old theories, for example, the Austrian School, J. B. Clark, and the Institutionalists."[42]

Blyumin mentioned the bourgeois opposition to Keynes but added "the overwhelming majority of bourgeois economists in the USA stand for state 'regulation' of the capitalist economy."[43] He held that the Truman and Eisenhower administrations followed Keynesian policies. He quoted Foster to the effect that the Republicans had adopted more Keynesian measures than the Roosevelt administration.[44]

In his concluding chapter, Blyumin concentrated on the battle the "progressive" economists were waging against Keynesianism. The economists, in this case communists such as Haywood, Anna Rochester, and Foster, among others, were discrediting Keynesianism and the illusions it created. This fight of the progressives was a theme that frequently appeared in the literature, and the Soviets presented this struggle as a counterweight to Keynesianism.[45]

It is interesting to note in this context what the Soviets had to say about the fight of the "progressives" in France, where Keynesian influences were also observed. E. Pletnev, in an article entitled "Progressive Economic Thought of France in the Fight Against Reactionary Ideology and Policy,"[46] reviewed the fight:

The most important direction of activity of the progressive economists in postwar France is the unmasking of Keynesian views and "theories" and of their adoption by the ruling classes in their practical policies. As one notices the passion of the French bourgeois ideologists and politicians for Keynesian theories about "state investment," "stable economy," "full

42. *Ibid.*, p. 74.
43. *Ibid.*, p. 75.   44. *Ibid.*, p. 86.
45. Another article on this point: Dmitriev, *Voprosy Ekonomiki*, 1955, No. 2, pp. 70–82.
46. E. Pletnev, "Progressivnaya ekonomicheskaya mysl Frantsii v borbe protiv reaktsionnoi ideologii i politiki," *Voprosy Ekonomiki*, 1955, No. 6, pp. 107–120.

employment," and so forth in the leading economic literature—this is not a short-term "fashion" but a reflection of the process of the further development of state-monopoly capitalism in the second stage of the general crisis of the world capitalist system.[47]

Later it was found that French political economy had undergone a change from Keynesianism. A. Pokrovskii, writing on "The Fate of Keynesianism in France,"[48] traced the movement from Keynesianism to *dirigisme*, which was defined as direct state intervention in the production process. Keynesianism, wrote Pokrovskii, was introduced in France in the late thirties and was well received despite minor criticisms:

> French bourgeois economists spoke enthusiastically of the "Keynesian revolution" and of the "renewal" of political economy, and so on. The penetration of Keynesianism in French political economy proceeded not only on the lines of an open apology for contemporary capitalism. A considerable part of the Keynesian theory was taken as the shield also by the theoreticians of the right-wing social democrats (J. Moch), who tried to use it in their futile attempts to revise Marxist-Leninist economic thought.[49]

Among the economists whom Pokrovskii considered to be Keynesians in addition to Jules Moch were Pierre Mendès-France and Gabriel Ardant; but the work of these Keynesians was in vain, according to Pokrovskii, because Keynesianism gave way to *dirigisme*:

> Beginning with the end of the 1940's and the early 1950's the relationship to the "great contemporary" sharply changed. A series of his basic theoretical positions (regulation of the interest rate, inflationary policies, and others) was repudiated. In the place of the "general theory," which limited the role of the state mainly to the sphere of monetary policy, theories were introduced that defend the principle of state interference directly in the production process. This principle received the name *dirigisme*.[50]

Such was the fate of Keynesianism in France according to the Soviets. Pokrovskii expanded his analysis into a book entitled *French*

47. *Ibid.*, p. 109.
48. A. Pokrovskii, "Sudba keinsianstva vo Frantsii," *Mirovaya Ekonomika i Mezhdunarodnye Otnosheniya*, 1959, No. 9, pp. 76–85.
49. *Ibid.*, p. 76.
50. *Ibid.* Another source on this topic: A. Aleksandrovskii, "Krizis burzhuaznoi ekonomicheskoi mysli vo Frantsii," *Voprosy Ekonomiki*, 1957, No. 3, pp. 80–92.

Bourgeois Political Economy,[51] which appeared in 1961. Here Po-krovskii enlarged on the development of *dirigisme* from Keynesian-ism, contending now that it was merely a revision of Keynesianism. The explanation offered was that both schools allowed state inter-vention, but *dirigisme* called for direct participation in the produc-tive process, whereas Keynesians only justified unproductive expen-ditures.[52] The French economists had criticized Keynes, but they had remained basically Keynesian and tried to reform him: "The revision of Keynesianism is witness to the attempts by bourgeois political economy to find new economic theories that would cor-respond to the changing conditions and demands of French capi-talism. *Dirigisme* is one of such theories."[53]

The Soviets were aware of Keynesian influence elsewhere in West-ern Europe, notably in West Germany and Austria. Dvorkin, in *A Critique of the Economic Theories of the Right-wing Socialists*,[54] recognized Keynesianism as the predominant influence in these two countries. He found that the right-wing socialists accepted Keynes-ianism as the natural supplement to the right-wing socialist theories of planning and organized capitalism. These views, he contended, were held in common with bourgeois economists of other countries: "Many reformist economists praise and propagandize the theory of Keynes. They call upon it as the means to save capitalism from crises and unemployment. Social democratic postwar programs are char-acterized by the fact that they . . . adapt many of Keynes's basic propositions to their own conditions."[55]

Dvorkin reviewed the programs of the social democrats in West Germany and Austria in the postwar years. Their emphasis on full employment was Keynesian. He upheld the usual argument that Keynesian inflationary policies only impoverished the workers, and that the law of absolute impoverishment was still in force.[56] He did not fail to mention the fight of the "progressives" who were leading the struggle against Keynesianism.

51. A. I. Pokrovskii, *Frantsuzskaya burzhuaznaya politicheskaya ekonomiya* (Moskva, 1961).
52. *Ibid.*, pp. 45–46.   53. *Ibid.*, p. 90.
54. I. N. Dvorkin, *Kritika ekonomicheskikh teorii pravykh sotsialistov, Zapadno-germanskikh i Avstriiskikh* (Moskva, 1959).
55. *Ibid.*, p. 297.   56. *Ibid.*, p. 174.

In regard to Germany, the Soviets tried to establish a connection between Keynes's theory and the policies of Hitlerite Germany. In his introductory article to the Russian edition of *The General Theory*, Blyumin recalled that Keynesian ideas had a favorable reception in German economic journals during Hitler's rule.[57] Also the Soviets frequently mentioned the preface to the German edition of *The General Theory*, in which Keynes observed that full employment would be easier to achieve in totalitarian conditions.[58] The Soviets distorted Keynes to the point where he was termed a reactionary and connected with fascist policies. It is true that Keynes had recognized that full employment could be realized by totalitarian systems, as it has in fact been realized by the Soviets. However, he never recommended such policies, but cautioned his readers that such methods were "at the expense of efficiency and freedom."[59]

The Socialist party of Austria was the subject of an article by I. Gladkov entitled "The Defense of Capitalism Under the Mask of 'Democratic Socialism.' "[60] Gladkov found the program of the socialists full of socialist phraseology and based on Keynesianism:

> It is not difficult to notice that this economic policy of the "democratic socialists" is based on Keynesianism—the fashionable bourgeois apologetic theory of "regulated" capitalism, of overcoming the cyclical development of capitalist economy and crises, of the lowering of unemployment, and even of guaranteeing "full employment" by means of regulating investment, credit, and the circulation of money.[61]

The Soviet writers found revisionism and Keynesianism in other countries as well. It was noticed in Australia by I. Markelev in his article "Battle Weapons in the Fight Against Revisionism."[62] Keynesianism was also found in Yugoslavia by A. Lobov-Sharonov, who maintained there was no difference in the positions of the English Labour party and the SKYu (League of Communists of Yugo-

57. Keins, *Teoriya*, p. xiii.
58. See, for example, Alter, *Krushenie teorii "planovogo kapitalizma,"* p. 97.
59. Keynes, *The General Theory*, p. 381.
60. I. Gladkov, "Zashchita kapitalizma pod maskoi 'demokratischeskogo sotsializma,' " *Voprosy Ekonomiki*, 1958, No. 1, pp. 66–78.
61. *Ibid.*, p. 69.
62. I. Markelev, "Boevoe oruzhie v borbe protiv revizionizma," *Voprosy Ekonomiki*, 1958, No. 12, pp. 139–140.

slavia).[63] Even Poland was tainted with Keynesian influences, according to Kozlov in his article mentioned earlier in this chapter, "The Triumph of the Theory of Scientific Communism."[64] Kozlov reviewed a number of attempts in the past by bourgeois ideologists to overthrow Marxism and save the capitalist system. He found Keynesianism at the basis of revisionism and at work in Poland:

The aim of revisionism is to subordinate the communist movement to the ideology of the right-wing socialists, who have gone over to the Keynesians in the field of economic theory. Some of the revisionists are fairly open about it. Recently in the Polish journal *Zhitse gospodarche* (No. 21, 1957), A. Sadovskii called for the demand to "enrich" Marxism by means of Keynesian theory. The miserable role of revisionism is apparent in that it opens the doors widely for bourgeois ideology to penetrate the ranks of the proletariat.[65]

The influence of Keynesian theory was seen to be international in scope. I. Mityurev in "The Theory of Full Employment and Reality"[66] discussed the measures taken against unemployment in the West. He alleged that real unemployment was two to three times greater than official unemployment in the United States.[67] In the introduction to his article Mityurev remarked that the term "full employment" was solidly embedded in the language of bourgeois politicians and economists. He mentioned that full employment was even a stated aim of political economy in a number of capitalist states. The United Nations Organization and the International Labor Organization had reviewed the problem of unemployment in relation to the Keynesian employment theory. Mityurev attributed this concept to Keynes: "At the foundation of this concept of full employment lies the general theory of employment, which was formulated by the English economist J. M. Keynes."[68]

The above references to Keynes and his influence were found principally in the leading economic journals and books published

63. A. Lobov-Sharonov, "Kritika burzhuaznoi sushchnosti leiborizma," *Sotsialisticheskii Trud*, 1959, No. 2, p. 158.

64. Kozlov, *Voprosy Ekonomiki*, 1958, No. 5, pp. 9–19.

65. *Ibid.*, p. 14.

66. I. Mityurev, "Teoriya polnoi zanyatosti i deistvitelnost," *Mirovaya Ekonomika i Mezhdunarodnye Otnosheniya*, 1960, No. 11, pp. 76–84.

67. *Ibid.*, p. 82.   68. *Ibid.*, p. 76.

by the various institutes of the Soviet Academy of Sciences. An indication that the spread of Keynesianism was giving cause for ever-greater concern was that references to Keynes and Keynesianism began to find their way into journals in other fields and into journals not merely in Moscow but also in outlying Soviet republics. An example of this was R. Ulyanovskii's article "Keynesianism or the Experience of the Socialist States" in *The Contemporary East*.[69] Ulyanovskii discussed India's second five-year plan and found that it gave too little emphasis to industrialization. He noticed two influences at work on the Indian economists, Marxist and Keynesian. Ulyanovskii stressed the Keynesian concept of socialization of investment:

> The assertion of Keynes that "sufficiently widespread socialization of investment" is the "only means to guarantee approximately full employment though this does not necessarily exclude all kinds of compromises and methods of co-operation of the state power with private initiative," has become the subject of numerous investigations.[70]

Ulyanovskii contended that Keynesianism created the illusion of full employment. He recommended to the Indian economists the experience of the socialist state where scientific theory and practice had eliminated unemployment. He noted the efforts of progressive Indian economists like Professor V. B. Singh who rejected Keynesianism as a means of solving the problem of industrialization for India and other underdeveloped countries.

The theme that so-called progressive economists were fighting Keynesianism was frequently used by Soviet writers in many different journals. In the majority of cases the views of these economists were seen only as they applied to the fight against Keynesianism in their particular countries. One notable exception was John Eaton, the English Marxist, whose book *Marx Against Keynes* was frequently quoted in the Soviet literature. Eaton's book was translated into Russian in 1958[71] and naturally received flattering reviews in the journals. Though the book was a Marxist answer to Herbert

69. R. Ulyanovskii, "Keinsianstvo ili opyt sotsialisticheskikh gosudarstv?" *Sovremennyi Vostok*, 1960, No. 7, pp. 27–29.

70. *Ibid.*, p. 28.

71. Dzh. Iton, *Marks protiv Keinsa*, trans. M. A. Menshikova (Moskva, 1958).

Morrison's definition of socialism,[72] the Soviets used it against all forms of revisionism and reformism, even the Yugoslavian.[73] In P. Oldak's review, "Keynesianism—the Theoretical Foundation of Contemporary Opportunism," *The General Theory* was referred to as the Bible of the opportunists.[74] S. Epshtein was of the same opinion in his review "Keynes—the Inspirer of Opportunism," in which Keynesianism was found to be bourgeois theory underlying opportunism.[75]

In the journals of various Soviet republics articles on Keynes dealing mainly with his influence on bourgeois economic thought started to appear in the late fifties. Keynesianism was attacked as the current economic theory of state monopoly capitalism. The arguments were similar to those found earlier in the leading economic journals, which probably served as models. As these were therefore largely repetitive of the themes already treated at some length, it seems unnecessary to give a detailed analysis of their contents. Among the journals that carried articles on Keynes were *Kommunist Ukrainy*,[76] *Kommunist Estonii*,[77] *Kommunist Sovtskoi Latvii*,[78] and *Izvestiya Akademiya Nauk Turkmenskoi SSR*.[79]

72. The reference here was to Herbert Morrison's speech at Perth on June 8, 1950, in which he defined socialism as "the assertion of social responsibility for matters which are properly of social concern" (John Eaton, *Marx Against Keynes*, [London, 1951], p. 7).

73. Lobov-Sharonov, *Sotsialisticheskii Trud*, 1959, No. 2, p. 158.

74. P. Oldak, *Mirovaya Ekonomika* . . . , 1960, No. 3, p. 129.

75. S. Epshtein, "Keins—vdokhnovitel opportunizma," *Novyi Mir*, 1959, No. 1, p. 265.

76. B. S. Kachura, "Vozmozhno li gosudarstvennoe regulirovanie khozyaistva v usloviyakh kapitalizma?," *Kommunist Ukrainy*, 1957, No. 8, pp. 62–70.

77. B. Mkrtchyan, " 'Levye' manipulyatsii burzhuaznykh ekonomistov," *Kommunist Estonii*, 1961, No. 4, pp. 75–83.

78. E. Mukin, "Keinsianstvo i ego reaktsionnaya sushchnost," *Kommunist Sovetskoi Latvii*, 1957, No. 5, pp. 69–74.

79. B. S. Kachura, "K voprosu o keinsianskikh teoriyakh stimuliruyushchego vliyaniya inflyatsii na promyshlennoe proizvodstvo SShA," *Izvestiya Akademii Nauk Turkmenskoi SSR*, 1950, No. 6, pp. 37–49. Kachura wrote a further article on Keynesianism in an Uzbekistan journal, "Keinsianskaya teoriya o 'reguliruemoi ekonomike'—otkrytyi prizyv k militarizatsii," *Kommunist Uzbekistana*, 1960, No. 10, n.v.

VII. *Keynes and the Khrushchev period*

The Twentieth Party Congress was the scene of Khrushchev's secret speech denouncing the personality cult of Stalin. The year 1956 also brought the dismissal of Molotov as foreign minister and the dissolution of the Cominform. These dramatic events helped to launch the campaign for peaceful coexistence that Khrushchev personally conducted throughout the years of his rule. Soviet writers maintained their interest in Keynes and Keynesianism throughout this period, and the relaxation of the harshness and arbitrariness of the Stalin period produced marked changes in many phases of Soviet life, including Soviet scholarship.

A significant revision appeared in Soviet ideology at this time. The Soviets now contended that a peaceful transition to socialism was possible. Khrushchev put the matter in this way:

> As to the forms of transition to socialism, they will become all the more varied as was pointed out by the Twentieth Congress of the CPSU. It is not binding as a result that the realization of the transition to socialism everywhere and in all cases will be connected with an armed uprising and civil war. Marxism-Leninism is based on the assumption that the forms of the transition to socialism can be peaceful or not peaceful.[1]

This altered official attitude brought a marked change on the part of the Soviets in the field of political economy.[2] In certain cases economists were now prepared to admit that some planning was possible in the capitalist system. Alter, for instance, answered the question as follows: "The essence of the question is that the bourgeois state with the help of the 'co-ordination of economic institutions' can regulate *only certain individual aspects* of economic life, sec-

1. N. S. Khrushchev, *O revolyutsionnom rabochem i kommunisticheskom dvizhenii* (Moskva, 1963), p. 37.
2. An example of this thaw: Gunnar Myrdal was invited to lecture at the Institute of Economics of the Academy of Sciences. See "Obsuzhdenie lekstii prof. G. Myrdalya 'teoriya stoimosti Rickardo,' " *Voprosy Ekonomiki*, 1957, No. 6, pp. 152–160.

tional processes which occur in the capitalist economy."[3] Alter identified Keynes with this planning on the part of the state. "The chief 'theoretical' basis of the contemporary policy of regulating the capitalist economy is Keynesianism,"[4] he asserted. He also pointed out that capitalist planning was not in the interest of the masses and that it was still subject to the erratic laws of capitalism.[5] Stalin was still quoted by Alter to the effect that it was impossible to direct the capitalist economy successfully.[6]

Professor Blyumin gave essentially the same analysis on the subject of planning in the capitalist system:

In the conditions of capitalism, the state can regulate only the private segments of the processes of the development of the economy (for example, the development of the military branches), but it is not in a position to regulate the total aggregate process of production of the social product and cannot control the national economy. This is explained by the fact that in any capitalist country, despite the introduction in several countries of partial nationalization of some branches of industry, the overwhelming mass of the means of production remains in the hands of the capitalists.[7]

Blyumin identified the Keynesian school with state intervention, planning, and the regulation of the economy.[8] He was also concerned with the distortion of socialist ideas by bourgeois economists:

In view of the great popularity of socialist ideas, the bourgeois ideologists have carried out a joint ideological maneuver: they establish the presence of socialism where there is not a speck of it (in the capitalist economy), and they deny its existence in the only place where it has its realization (in the socialist countries). This remarkable *qui* [*sic*] *pro quo* demonstrates those tricks and turns which the contemporary bourgeois apology is forced to take in its attempt to show that it is not hostile to socialist ideas.[9]

Blyumin was joined by Dvorkin in a book entitled *The Myth*

3. L. B. Alter, *Kritika teorii "reguliruemogo kapitalizma"* (Moskva, 1957), p. 11.
4. *Ibid.*, p. 12. 5. *Ibid.*, pp. 11–12.
6. *Ibid.*, p. 40. The reference was to Stalin, *Sochineniya*, X, 326.
7. I. G. Blyumin, "O krizise sovremennoi burzhuaznoi politicheskoi ekonomii," *Voprosy Ekonomiki*, 1957, No. 12, p. 70. A similar article on this theme was A. Rubinshtein, "Chto skryvaetsya za reformistskimi 'teoriyami' vtoroi promyshlennoi revolutsii," *Voprosy Ekonomiki*, 1957, No. 12, pp. 76–89.
8. Blyumin, *Voprosy Ekonomiki*, 1957, No. 12, p. 66.
9. *Ibid.*, p. 73.

about Peoples' Capitalism,[10] in which these authors continued the theme of capitalist planning. A new spirit of inquiry was in evidence as they admitted that capitalism had outwardly changed:

It is understood that it would be completely incorrect to compare like two drops of water modern capitalism and capitalism as it was say one hundred years ago. During these hundred years the capitalist economy has undergone real changes. The question is not whether capitalism has changed in the middle of the twentieth century in comparison with capitalism of the last century. The whole question is *what is the outcome of these changes.*[11]

The authors reviewed a series of bourgeois theories concerning capitalism and gave much emphasis to the theory of capitalism without crisis. Keynes was credited by the authors as the bourgeois economist who developed the theoretical base for the regulation of the economy of crisis-free capitalism.[12] The authors concluded that capitalism, in essence, had not changed and that it could not escape its inherent contradictions. However, there was no reference to Stalin on this point. Instead, Khrushchev was now quoted.[13] In addition, the authors introduced criticisms of the Keynesian theory by Haberler and Fellner, which was in marked contrast to criticisms at the height of the cold war period, when as a rule only Western communists were quoted.

During the early part of this period there was considerable overlap. Many works were still written in the harsh tones of the cold war. These still stressed military expenditures and called for the unmasking of Keynes in this connection.[14] In 1958 the *Concise Economic Dictionary* still pictured Keynes in these terms:

Keynes, John Maynard (1883–1946)—English bourgeois economist who greatly influenced contemporary bourgeois economic science. The ideologist of monopoly capitalism and imperialist reaction. . . . The class essence of Keynes's position was exhaustively revealed back in 1920 by Lenin. In Lenin's estimate, Keynes was "an avowed bourgeois, a ruthless

---

10. I. G. Blyumin and I. N. Dvorkin, *Mif o narodnom kapitalizme* (Moskva, 1957).
11. *Ibid.*, pp. 8–9.
12. *Ibid.*, p. 98.　　　　13. *Ibid.*, p. 97.
14. R. Khafizov, "Mif o 'reguliruemoi ekonomike' kapitalizma i neizbezhnost ekonomicheskikh krizisov," *Voprosy Ekonomiki*, 1957, No. 6, pp. 114–120.

opponent of bolshevism, which he, as an English philistine, pictures in an ugly, savage, and brutal manner" (V. I. Lenin, *Works*, Vol. 31, p. 195).[15]

The above example, however, was not typical of the literature of the period. At the height of the cold war the Soviets concentrated on Keynes and criticized his theory. They did so at the expense of other theories existing in the West. During the Khrushchev period the Soviets rediscovered these theories and wrote extensively on them. Further, the Soviets now admitted of variations among the Keynesians, whereas previously only one interpretation of Keynesianism had been allowed.

In their joint work, Blyumin and Dvorkin discussed the following theories in addition to Keynesianism: the democratization of capital, the managerial revolution, the equality of incomes, peoples' capitalism, and the theory of countervailing power. This last theory was identified with Galbraith, who saw other organizations opposing and neutralizing the power of monopoly and big business. The authors objected to Galbraith and maintained that trade unions in particular would effect only "a small weakening of the encroachment on the living standards of the working class."[16] Later, S. Dalin thought that Galbraith had tried to see the essence of the capitalist development but had failed.[17] Galbraith, in Dalin's opinion, was a pupil of Keynes but "appeared as a non-orthodox Keynesian long ago by giving his own theory of state intervention in economic life."[18]

Blyumin in his *On Contemporary Bourgeois Political Economy*[19] dealt with a wide variety of schools and theories: regulated capitalism, free enterprise, neo-Malthusianism, fascism, and the theory of competition and distribution. He concentrated on the regulated capitalism and free enterprise schools. He designated the school of regulated capitalism as Keynesian and found it to be predominant.[20] Blyumin gave considerable attention to the neo-liberals or the free

15. Koslov and Pervushin, eds., *Kratkii ekonomicheskii slovar*, pp. 122–123.
16. Blyumin and Dvorkin, *Mif o narodnom kapitalizme*, p. 89.
17. S. Dalin, "Prodolzhenie legendy," *Mirovaya Ekonomika i Mezhdunarodnye Otnosheniya*, 1963, No. 8, pp. 142–145.
18. *Ibid.*, p. 142.
19. I. G. Blyumin, *O sovremennoi burzhuaznoi politicheskoi ekonomii* (Moskva, 1958).
20. *Ibid.*, p. 31.

enterprise school and discussed the works of Eucken, Roepke, von Mises, and David McCord Wright.

Likewise M. Ya. Volkov reviewed a number of theories in his *Contemporary Bourgeois Political Economy of England,*[21] including the theory of imperfect competition and the theory of general prosperity. Volkov found that Keynes's theory provided the main theoretical basis for English political economy.[22] However, he recognized the influence of neo-liberal theories:

In the light of the reaction to the sudden growth of neo-Keynesian theories, recently in England various theories of neo-liberalism that attempt to adapt the theoretical dogmas of pre-Keynesian bourgeois political economy to new conditions have become widespread.

The English neo-liberals maintain that state interference in the economy hinders automatic regulation and at the same time forces the economy in the direction that is neither the most rational nor correct.[23]

In a work on *Monopoly Capitalism-Imperialism*[24] by the Institute of International Relations of the Academy of Sciences, Keynesianism was recognized as the leading theory of the West and Keynes's influence was particularly noted in regard to employment theory. Other theories, especially the theory of mixed capitalism and neo-liberalism, were also discussed. Neo-liberalism continued to receive attention and was the subject of an article by V. Kotov entitled "The Neo-liberal School in Contemporary Bourgeois Political Economy."[25] Kotov acknowledged Keynes as the person who broke the tradition of liberalism. He found that the neo-liberals were taking issue with the Keynesians over full employment and inflation and remarked that the neo-liberals were generally against state intervention in the economy except when intervention was against the workers.[26]

In a review of B. Seligman's *Main Currents in Modern Econom-*

21. M. Ya.Volkov, *Sovremennaya burzhuazhnaya politicheskaya ekonomiya Anglii* (Moskva, 1963).

22. *Ibid.,* p. 15.   23. *Ibid.,* pp. 19–20.

24. E. Ya. Bregel, ed., *Monopolisticheskii kapitalizm-imperializm* (Moskva, 1961).

25. V. Kotov, "Neoliberalnoye napravleniye v sovremennoi burzhuaznoi politekonomii," *Voprosy Ekonomiki,* 1961, No. 4, pp. 45–58.

26. *Ibid.,* p. 58.

ics (New York, 1963),[27] R. Mikhailov agreed with Seligman that Keynes was the founder of the macroeconomic school. Mikhailov also drew attention to the Chicago school in this book: "One of the famous representatives of this school, M. Friedman, claims that state regulation 'threatens individual freedom.' "[28] Ryndina also recognized Keynes as the father of macroeconomic theories, but she maintained that macroeconomics had not advanced the cause of bourgeois economic science.[29] Her explanation for this assertion was that the "Keynesians consider that the reason for unemployment of people and resources is the insufficiency of demand for goods. But this insufficient demand is only an outward form of the manifestation of a crisis and cannot be the reason for the latter. The crisis itself demands an explanation."[30]

In many Soviet works Keynes's influence was recognized but there was no lengthy treatment of *The General Theory*. Keynes would be acknowledged as the leader, father, founder, or ideologist; and then the Soviets would proceed to treat the work of his followers or the areas where his influence was felt. A. Russkikh, in "The Crisis of Bourgeois Economic Thought in Contemporary France,"[31] found that Keynesianism had been modified in France because of the shortage of capital and the fear of inflation. S. M. Nikitin, in his "Criticism of Economic Theories of 'Planning' of the Capitalist Economy,"[32] contended that econometrics was heavily influenced by Keynes's theory. Oldak, in an article "On the Criticism of the Contemporary Keynesian Conception of the Economic Cycle,"[33] dealt with Hansen's development of Keynes's ideas on the business

27. R. Mikhailov, "Kniga o sovremennoi burzhuaznoi politicheskoi ekonomii," *Mirovaya Ekonomika i Mezhdunarodnye Otnosheniya*, 1964, No. 9, pp. 141–145.
28. *Ibid.*, p. 144.
29. M. Ryndina, "Antinauchaya metodologiya sovremennoi burzhuaznoi politicheskoi ekonomii," *Voprosy Ekonomiki*, 1963, No. 10, pp. 74–87.
30. *Ibid.*, p. 84.
31. A. Russkikh, "Krizis burzhuaznoi ekonomicheskoi mysli sovremennoi Frantsii," *Voprosy Ekonomiki*, 1962, No. 3, pp. 136–139.
32. S. M. Nikitin, *Kritika ekonomicheskikh teorii "planirovaniya" kapitalisticheskoi ekonomiki* (Moskva, 1962), pp. 15, 45.
33. P. Oldak, "K kritike sovremennoi keinsianskoi kontseptsii ekonomicheskogo tsikla," *Mirovaya Ekonomika i Mezhdunarodnye Otnosheniya*, 1960, No. 3, pp. 128–141.

cycle. Cheprakov, writing on "Contemporary Capitalism and Anti-Marxism,"[34] found that the anti-Marxists had borrowed their theory chiefly from Keynes. The Soviet literature on the followers of Keynes becomes voluminous during the period under review.[35]

Although the Soviets mentioned other schools of bourgeois economic theory, the school of the regulated economy or state intervention was invariably recognized as the predominant one, and was generally referred to as Keynesian. Khafizov, in his *Criticism of the Theory of the Regulation of the Capitalist Economy*, published in 1961, held that Keynes's theory was the basic theory of the state regulation of the capitalist economy.[36] Alter surveyed political economy in the United States and found that Keynesianism was the leading school.[37] Dalin was of the opinion that state intervention in the economy was a necessity for capitalism following the crises of 1929–1933 and declared: "The father of this school is Keynes. To a known degree this is correct, for all the present supporters of state intervention have joined Keynes in their time."[38]

Though Keynesianism was recognized as the predominant school, the Soviets found that it was being challenged. I. Naimov reported on the papers delivered at a conference (no dates given) at the Academy of Sciences that criticized the newest bourgeois theories.[39] At this conference Alter's paper concluded that Keynesianism was in crisis, and he singled out the following elements in the struggle: the

34. V. Cheprakov, "Sovremennyi kapitalizm i antimarksizm," *Kommunist*, 1957, No. 17, pp. 65–82.

35. A representative selection: I. G. Blyumin, ed., *Kritika teorii reguliruemogo kapitalizma* (Moskva, 1959); M. N. Ryndina, ed., *Kritika burzhuaznykh ekonomicheskikh teorii* (Moskva, 1960); V. I. Dolukin and V. P. Trepelkov, *Obshchii krizis kapitalizma* (Moskva, 1963); L. I. Glukharev, *O sovremennom gosudarstvenno—monopolisticheskom kapitalizme* (Moskva, 1963); G. Khromushin, "Antikommunizm—glavnoe soderzhanie ideologii imperializma," *Voprosy Ekonomiki*, 1963, No. 8, pp. 43–52.

36. R. Kh. Khafizov, *Kritika teorii gosudarstvennogo regulirovaniya kapitalisticheskoi ekonomiki* (Moskva, 1961), p. 29.

37. L. B. Alter, *Burzhuaznaya politicheskaya ekonomiya SShA* (Moskva, 1961), p. 562.

38. S. Dalin, "Ekonomicheskaya teoriya amerikanskogo rante," *Mirovaya Ekonomika i Mezhdunarodnye Otnosheniya*, 1964, No. 10, p. 61.

39. I. Naimov, "K kritike sovremennoi burzhuaznoi politekonomii," *Mirovaya Ekonomika i Mezhdunarodnye Otnosheniya*, 1964, No. 8, pp. 140–144.

extreme right, Keynesians and economic growth, radical Keynesians, and the anti-monopoly petty bourgeois position.[40] In a later article Alter found that Keynesianism had been influenced considerably by the supporters of the free enterprise school who preached limitation in government activity.[41] Cheprakov saw Keynesianism struggling to maintain its position:

> And a struggle, a real struggle between the schools of monopoly capitalism is being waged over the question as to which methods ought to be adopted to save the decaying capitalist system. In a survey of this struggle one can schematically divide the economists of monopoly capitalism into two groups: one group—the followers of Keynes, the other—those who assume the name of neo-liberals in Western Europe but are called representatives of economic conservatism in the USA.[42]

The Soviets were constantly finding new theories of bourgeois economy and were quick to disprove them. At the end of the period under review, greatest attention was paid to the theory of growth or dynamics. The Soviets maintained that this theory was an outgrowth of Keynesianism, which was too static for the conditions of the battle between the socialist and the capitalist systems during the general crisis of capitalism, which had now entered its third stage, distinguished from the previous stages in that it occurred without a world war.[43]

Alter took this new stage as a starting point for his criticism "On the Newest Bourgeois Theory of 'Economic Growth.'"[44] He began with a statement of the Communist and Workers' Parties' Declaration, which noted the instability of the capitalist economy. Alter found this instability in bourgeois political economy as well:

> This estimate must be applied foremost to Keynesianism, which is the main school of bourgeois political economy in the epoch of the general

40. *Ibid.*, p. 141.
41. L. B. Alter, "Teoriya i praktika kapitalisticheskogo regulirovaniya," *Mirovaya Ekonomika i Mezhdunarodnye Otnosheniya*, 1964, No. 3, p. 65.
42. V. Cheprakov, "Gosudarstvenno-monopolisticheskii kapitalizm i burzhuaznaya politicheskaya ekonomiya," *Voprosy Ekonomiki*, 1962, No. 7, p. 95.
43. In November, 1960, representatives from eighty-one Communist and Workers' parties met in Moscow and defined this new third stage of capitalism. For the complete statement of their findings see *Pravda*, Dec. 6, 1960, pp. 1–4.
44. L. Alter, "O noveishei burzhuaznoi teorii 'ekonomicheskogo rosta,'" *Voprosy Ekonomiki*, 1961, No. 6, pp. 84–98.

crisis of capitalism. The failure of the Keynesian program, which set it-self the unrealistic task of eliminating the anarchy of capitalist production and of saving capitalism from economic crises and of preserving the capitalist social system at the same time, is one of the indications of the deep crisis in contemporary bourgeois policy and ideology.

In these conditions of bourgeois political economy there is an attempt to find new forms of apologetics and new means of "saving" capitalism. However, as formerly, the matter leads only to some deformation and adaptation of old, vulgar theories to the changing historical conditions. On the one hand, in bourgeois political economy anti-Keynesian trends that demand a return to "Say's Law" are strengthening, and, on the other hand, there are definite movements in the camp of the Keynesians themselves that attempt to renovate the theory and methods of Keynes and adapt them to the conditions of the new stage of the general crisis of capitalism.

The strengthening of the influence of the so-called theory of "economic growth" serves as the most significant expression of the evolution in bourgeois political economy in recent years.[45]

Alter noted that Keynesianism was a static theory and was concerned with unemployment and the depression of the thirties. Unemployment, Alter continued, was still a problem, but the bourgeois economists had to force the pace of economic growth as a result of the competition with socialism. Hence the concentration on the theory of growth. Alter noted two schools of growth. He reviewed briefly the works of Harrod and Domar as representing one form and found that they had accepted a number of basic propositions of Keynes's theory such as the propensities and the multiplier.[46] Rostow was given as an example of the second form, classified as the sociological school. Both schools, Alter found, would have no success as the competition was decided in favor of the socialist system.

In a study entitled *The Criticism of Contemporary Bourgeois Reformist and Revisionist Economic Theories* by Z. N. Belyaeva and V. A. Budarin,[47] the theory of the regulated economy was held as the most representative for the first and second stages of the general crisis of capitalism. They contended: "The main representative of

45. *Ibid.*, p. 84.   46. *Ibid.*, p. 85.
47. Z. N. Belyaeva and V. A. Budarin, *Kritika sovremennykh burzhuaznykh reformistskikh i revizionistskikh ekonomicheskikh teorii* (Moskva, 1962).

this school is the English bourgeois economist J. M. Keynes."[48] In the third stage of the crisis, the authors found, the growth theories were representative of the capitalist attempt to reply to the great successes of the socialist economy.[49]

Dvorkin also dealt with the theory of growth.[50] Basically he agreed with the above writers on growth. Keynesianism had been the theory after World War II and had then given way to growth theory that Dvorkin called neo-Keynesian: "The transition from Keynesian policy of 'full employment' to the neo-Keynesian theory of growth reflected the intention of the bourgeois economists to strengthen the position of capitalism by means of the exertion of state influence on the rate of growth of production in the competition between the two systems."[51] Dvorkin found that Keynesianism was constantly being challenged. Prior to the third stage of capitalism's general crisis, the struggle had largely been between the Keynesians and the partisans of free enterprise. Now, in Dvorkin's opinion, the battle was between the Keynesian and non-Keynesian theories of state intervention.[52]

Other Soviet economists took an interest in the theory of growth and dynamics. They recognized Keynes's theory as the major influence on growth. I. Osadchaya gave Harrod the credit for the theory of dynamics, but she noted: "The majority of the supporters of the theory of economic dynamics belong to the school of bourgeois political economy that is called Keynesian."[53] S. L. Vygodskii, in his *Sketch of the Theory of Contemporary Capitalism*, directly related the theory of growth to Keynesianism.[54] Pokrovskii found that economic growth models grew from the Keynesian model.[55] S. A. Khavina reviewed the criticisms of Keynesianism advanced by the sup-

48. *Ibid.*, p. 11.   49. *Ibid.*, p. 21.
50. I. N. Dvorkin, "Ekonomicheskoe sorevnovanie dvykh sistem i sovremennaya burzhuaznaya politicheskaya ekonomiya," *Voprosy Ekonomiki*, 1964, No. 10, pp. 99–110.
51. *Ibid.*, p. 106.   52. *Ibid.*, p. 107.
53. I. Osadchaya, "Po povody sovremennykh burzhuaznykh teorii ekonomicheskoi dinamiki," *Voprosy Ekonomiki*, 1958, No. 10, p. 91.
54. S. L. Vygodskii, *Ocherki teorii sovremennogo kapitalizma* (Moskva, 1961), pp. 233–241.
55. A. I. Pokrovskii, *Frantsuzskaya burzhuaznaya politicheskaya ekonomiya* (Moskva, 1961), p. 147.

porters of the growth theory, but she maintained that the growth theory borrowed heavily from the Keynesian one.[56]

Osadchaya produced yet another variation in the classification of the theories of growth in her *Criticism of Contemporary Theories of Economic Growth*.[57] She found three broad categories of growth, which she named the Keynesian, the left-Keynesian, and the sociological theories.[58] Harrod, Kaldor, and Hicks were given as representatives of the Keynesian school; Joan Robinson represented the left-Keynesians; and Walt W. Rostow, W. A. Lewis, Bert F. Hoselitz, and Joseph Spengler were among those representing the sociological school. She did not cover theories especially constructed for underdeveloped countries, as she maintained this was a special area of the bourgeois theory of growth and therefore needed separate investigation.[59]

The Soviets continued to link Keynes with revisionist and reformist theories throughout this period. Dvorkin found that present reformism was an open and direct enemy of Marxism, whereas early reformism of the late nineteenth and early twentieth century was hidden under Marxian terminology.[60] Keynesianism was used by the present reformist groups: "After World War II Keynesian ideas of state regulation of capital investment and 'full employment' were accepted by all social democratic parties of Western Europe and were built into the foundations of their program."[61] However, Kozlov in an article commemorating Marx's birthday found revisionists still clothing themselves in Marxist terms but adopting Keynesianism at the same time:

> Revisionists demand a departure from Leninism to "Marxism." In this there is hidden nothing other than a departure from Marxism because Leninism is Marxism in our epoch—the epoch of the march from capi-

---

56. S. A. Khavina, *Protiv burzhuaznykh ekonomicheskikh psevdoteorii sotsializma* (Moskva, 1962), p. 178.

57. I. Osadchaya, *Kritika sovremennykh burzhauznykh teorii ekonomicheskogo rosta* (Moskva, 1963).

58. *Ibid.*, p. 2.   59. *Ibid.*, p. 18.

60. I. N. Dvorkin, "Reaktsionnaya sushchnost sovremennogo reformizma," *Voprosy Ekonomiki*, 1957, No. 6, p. 93.

61. *Ibid.*, p. 94.

talism to socialism, the epoch of the creation of the world socialist system of economy. Only in Leninism has Marxism received its real scientific development. Revisionists and reformists, who press the demand for a turn from Leninism "in the name of Marxism," follow the goal of opening the way to exchange Marxism for the theory of Keynes.[62]

Regulated capitalism, or Keynesianism, in the opinion of the Soviets, served as the basis for social democratic and reformist groups. Ryndina, in her study of revisionism, stated that "reformists proclaim the Keynesian conception of 'regulated capitalism' as the theoretical basis of 'democratic socialism.' "[63] Kh. Momdzhyan noted that the reformists had shifted to the right and had taken regulated capitalism from Keynes to mean socialism.[64]

M. N. Smit in her history of bourgeois political economy dealt mainly with revisionist movements.[65] She analyzed Keynesianism and admitted its influence but recognized the influence of others in the West.[66] G. P. Solyus[67] found that right-wing socialists and revisionists repeated what bourgeois economists wrote. Solyus remarked, however: "Bourgeois economists who defend capitalism are not ashamed to say that they stand on the position of capitalism, whereas the right-wing opportunists who fulfil these same tasks of defending capitalism make it somehow appear as the position of socialists."[68] He claimed that bourgeois theoreticians seized the Keynesian idea of state intervention as the "anchor of salvation," though they rejected many other of the Keynesian ideas.[69] He did not elaborate on Keynes and

62. G. Kozlov, "Torzhestvo teorii nauchnogo kommunizma," *Voprosy Ekonomiki*, 1958, No. 5, p. 18.

63. M. N. Ryndina, *Kritika ekonomicheskikh teorii revizionistov* (Moskva, 1960), p. 28. Also N. A. Tsagolov, ed., *Kritika sovremennykh burzhuaznykh reformistskikh i revizionistskikh ekonomicheskikh teorii* (Moskva, 1960), p. 38; F. Polyanskii, "Kritika burzhuaznykh, reformistskikh i revizionistskikh teorii," *Voprosy Ekonomiki*, 1960, No. 9, pp. 102–107.

64. Kh. Momdzhyan, "Dalneishii sdvig vpravo v ideologii sovremennogo reformizma," *Kommunist*, 1960, No. 3, p. 91.

65. M. N. Smit, *Ocherki istorii burzhuaznoi politicheskoi ekonomii* (Moskva, 1961).

66. *Ibid.*, p. 293; Also A. P. Mamalui, ed., *Kritika sovremennykh burzhuaznykh reformistskikh i revizionistskikh teorii po voprosam politicheskoi ekonomii* (Kharkov, 1963), pp. 137–138.

67. G. P. Solyus, *Razvitie gosudarstvenno-monopolisticheskogo kapitalizma v usloviyakh obshchego krizisa kapitalizma* (Moskva, 1963).

68. *Ibid.*, p. 77.   69. *Ibid.*, p. 74.

concentrated mainly on Keynes's followers in the leading capitalist countries.

During this period the Soviets continued to stress the influence of Keynes on England and especially on the Labour party. G. Khromushin, in his criticism of "English Laborites Today," stressed the point that "the entire program of Gaitskell is none other than Keynesianism somewhat prettified."[70] In reference to the British Labour party, Blyumin, in a further article, came to the conclusion that Keynesianism was a fundamental part of its program:

In the Labour literature there are propagated everywhere the propositions and conclusions of Keynes. Thus the formulation of the problem of full employment is given from the clearly Keynesian position, and the slogan for the creation of capitalism without crises is issued as a consequence of state financing of all means of public expenditures.[71]

M. K. Bunkina concluded her analysis of the right-wing socialist theory of the peaceful evolution of capitalism into socialism thus: "The economic theory of Keynes is above all the reservoir that feeds the 'newest' right-wing socialist concoctions of this question. Keynesianism is at the basis of the platforms of the leading ideologists of the English social democrats . . . ."[72] In discussing British laborites, the Soviets would give more attention to current figures such as John Strachey and Douglas Jay after acknowledging their debt to Keynes. I. Pustovalov restricted Keynesian influence to England in his article and reviewed Strachey's works.[73] I. Dvorkin was of the opinion that Douglas Jay's theory in which capitalism's ills were due to free competition was similar to Strachey's and hence based on Keynes's theory of the regulation of the economy by the state.[74]

70. G. Khromushin, "Angliiskie leiboristy segodnya," *Nauchnye Doklady Vysshei Shkoly*, Ekonomicheskie Nauki, 1959, No. 1, p. 183.

71. I. G. Blyumin, *Istoriya ekonomicheskikh uchenii* (Moskva, 1961), pp. 252–253.

72. M. K. Bunkina, *Kritika pravosotsialisticheskoi teorii "vrastaniya" kapitalizma v sotsializm* (Moskva, 1961), p. 12.

73. I. Pustovalov, "Sovremennaya burzhuaznaya politekonomiya na sluzhbe monopolisticheskogo kapitala," *Voprosy Ekonomiki*, 1963, No. 5, pp. 50–61. Another article on Keynes's influence on Strachey was V. Motylev, "Sovremennyi kapitalizm v krivom zerkale reformistskoi teorii Dzhona Strechi," *Nauchnye Doklody Vysshei Shkoly*, Ekonomicheskie Nauki, 1962, No. 4, pp. 54–65.

74. I. N. Dvorkin, "Pravoleiboristskii variant teorii neo-kapitalizma," *Mirovaya Ekonomika i Mezhdunarodnye Otnosheniya*, 1963, No. 6, pp. 144–148.

A few Soviet writers even found Keynesianism influencing both the Conservative and Labour parties in England. The University of Moscow's study, *The Sources of Contemporary Revisionism and Its Bourgeois Essence*, was of this opinion.[75] Writers also found the Kennedy administration following neo-Keynesian policies. One writer, Shundeev, quoted an October issue of *The New Republic* to the effect that a new Keynes was necessary in the United States.[76] Shundeev maintained that the original Keynesianism was bankrupt and a new Keynes and new Keynesian theory did not exist.[77]

There was no point-for-point rebuttal of *The General Theory* during this period, but several works treated certain aspects of Keynes's theory. E. Bregel wrote on Keynes's concept of inflation which, he maintained, had been adopted by many bourgeois economists.[78] Bregel outlined Keynes's definition of inflation correctly but found it inadequate. He warned of the social and economic consequences of inflation that would result if Keynesian ideas of monetary and credit therapy were applied to cure the diseases of unemployment and crisis: "Keynes sees as one of the chief reasons for unemployment the limited quantity of money, which, in his words, calls forth a high level of interest rate, which, in turn, limits the amount of investment and thereby the level of employment."[79]

Keynesianism was also held responsible for fiscal policy measures in the capitalist countries. R. Entov reviewed theories of deficit finance and the growing national debt in the United States, England, France, and Italy, and gave Keynes the honor of formulating the theory behind these policies.[80] Yu. Olsevich found that the

75. F. Ya. Polyanskii, ed., *Istoki sovremennogo revizionizma i ego burzhuaznaya sushchnost* (Moskva, 1961), p. 372; also N. Yarovoi, "Keinsianskie retsepty dlya poslevoennoi ekonomicheskoi politiki Anglii," *Mirovaya Ekonomika i Mezhdunarodnye Otnosheniya*, 1959, No. 4, pp. 152–155.

76. V. Shundeev, "Ob ekonomicheskoi politike Kennedi," *Mirovaya Ekonomika i Mezhdunarodnye Otnosheniya*, 1963, No. 6, p. 58.

77. *Ibid.*, p. 69.

78. E. Bregel, "Sovremennye burzhuaznye i reformistskie teorii inflyatsii," *Voprosy Ekonomiki*, 1959, No. 4, pp. 91–105.

79. *Ibid.*, p. 102. See also E. Varga, *Sovremennyi kapitalizm i ekonomicheskie krizisy* (Moskva, 1963), pp. 479–481.

80. R. Entov, "Sovremennye keinsianskie teorii defitsitnogo finansirovaniya i mif o 'demokratizatsii gosudarstvennogo dolga,'" *Voprosy Ekonomiki*, 1960, No. 10, pp. 54–64.

proponents of military spending availed themselves of Keynesian policies:

With the expansion of parasitic military consumption the policies and ideologists of capitalism intend to "speed" the tempo of capitalist reproduction. They base themselves above all on the Keynesian formula of deficit finance, which contends that state loans help mobilize so-called "surplus" capital and use this surplus power for an increase in production.[81]

A. Miroshnikov reviewed the classical theory of saving and the Keynesian theory based on the fundamental psychological law that saving occurs with increased income.[82] Since Keynes had attacked surplus savings, his theory had been viewed as "leftist" and had been accepted by the laborites.[83] Miroshnikov found workers did very little saving and objected to Keynes's viewing saving in the aggregate.

The new philosophy and the new orthodox theory of government debt were reviewed by M. Bogachevskii, who maintained that these new philosophies concerning the debt were a reworking of Malthus and Lauderdale.[84] Bogachevskii stated that Keynes had advocated pump-priming measures before the appearance of *The General Theory*, but had proposed compensating expenditures in this book as an anti-crisis measure. He attributed the new theories of expanding fiscal policy and increased debt to Keynes. In his conclusions, he saw the rich benefiting at the expense of the poor as a result of such policies. He estimated the debt of certain Western countries in rubles and then gave his readers an indication of what such wealth would buy in the Soviet Union in the way of schools, hospitals, flats, and other social items.[85]

Gold was another topic of concern to the Soviets, and O. Bog-

81. Yu. Olsevich, "Kapitalisticheskoe vosproizvodstvo i militarizatsiya ekonomiki," *Voprosy Ekonomiki*, 1962, No. 2, p. 88.

82. A. Miroshnikov, "Reaktsionaya sushchnost keinsianskoi teorii 'chrezmernykh' ili 'neklassicheskikh' sberezhenii," *Nauchnye Doklady Vysshei Shkoly*, Ekonomicheskie Nauki, 1958, No. 2, pp. 88–102.

83. *Ibid.*, pp. 89–90.

84. M. Bogachevskii, "Burzhuaznaya apologetika pod vidom 'noveishei teorii' gosudarstvennogo kredita," *Finansy SSSR*, 1963, No. 7, p. 44.

85. *Ibid.*, p. 48.

danov reviewed the position of the capitalist countries with respect to it.[86] His findings showed that gold had lost its significance in the West but that this trend would lead to difficulties and crises:

Contemporary bourgeois political economy does all that it can to lower and lessen the significance of gold in the sphere of money exchange in the capitalist countries and in their international accounts. Following Keynes, who called gold nothing other than a "barbarous relic," the apologists of state-monopoly capitalism set their hopes on the possibility of "regulating" finances by means of manipulating only paper money exchange without regard to any connection with the availability of gold and the quantity of gold reserves.[87]

Unemployment remained a favorite target of the Soviet writers during this period. As in other areas concerning Keynes, the Soviets noticed more recent developments and were more flexible in their criticism. E. Bregel's article on "Contemporary Bourgeois Theories of Unemployment" is a case in point.[88] He listed four main theories of unemployment, one of which was the theory of insufficient demand, attributed to Keynes: "The theory of unemployment of the English economist J. M. Keynes, which can be labeled the theory of insufficient demand, is the most widespread in contemporary bourgeois political economy."[89] Bregel discussed Keynes's followers, particularly those in the United States, in connection with this theory.

I. Mityurev discussed the Keynesian theory as it was developed by Alvin Hansen and A. P. Lerner and found that these theories had failed to solve the problem, since unemployment still existed in the West.[90] V. Goilo was of the opinion that the new schools of bourgeois economics were not concerned with unemployment as were Keynesians:

The devoted followers of Keynesianism attempt to prove the possibility of liquidating mass unemployment and establishing "full employment"

86. O. Bogdanov, "Zoloto v finansovoi sisteme imperializma," *Mirovaya Ekonomika i Mezhdunarodnye Otnosheniya*, 1963, No. 8, pp. 63–72.
87. *Ibid.*, p. 63.
88. E. Bregel, "Sovremennye burzhuaznye teorii bezrabotitsy," *Mirovaya Ekonomika i Mezhdunarodnye Otnosheniya*, 1958, No. 7, pp. 78–93.
89. *Ibid.*, p. 90.
90. I. Mityurev, "Teoriya polnoi zanyatosti i deistvitelnost," *Mirovaya Ekonomika i Mezhdunarodnye Otnosheniya*, 1960, No. 11, pp. 76–87.

in the conditions of the capitalist system. Neo-liberals and supporters of the theory of so-called dynamic growth—the right-wing Keynesians—consider that the problem of unemployment does not face capitalism . . . . They not only recommend keeping to unemployment but are also not afraid of its growth.[91]

M. G. Guttsait, in a full-length work entitled *Chronic Unemployment and Idle Enterprises in the USA,* reviewed various theories of employment starting with the Pigou-Keynes controversy over voluntary unemployment.[92] Guttsait found all these theories unacceptable. Although the position of the Soviet writers on unemployment had not altered greatly, they discussed the subject in a less vindictive tone than had the earlier Soviet writers. This was indeed a marked change from economists like D. I. Valentei, who wrote at the height of the cold war.[93]

Keynes and his theory found their way into Soviet university textbooks on political economy and economic thought during this period. A program for a course entitled History of Economic Thought contained the following outline:

Vulgar bourgeois political economy of England. J. M. Keynes as the apologist of state-monopoly capitalism. V. I. Lenin on Keynes. The work of Keynes, *The General Theory of Employment, Interest and Money,* its anti-Marxist, reactionary theme. The bankruptcy of Keynesian methodology. The unmasking of the theory of "employment" of J. M. Keynes. The apologetic interpretation of "forced unemployment" and economic crises.

The criticism of the theory of "regulated capitalism" of Keynes. The attempts of the ways of "restoring" capitalism to health and guaranteeing high monopoly profits in the conditions of the general crisis of capitalism. Reactionary militaristic character of the program of the economic policy of Keynes. The Keynesian basis for the encroachment on the living standards and political rights of the proletariat, the parasitic consumption of the bourgeoisie, and the militarization of the economy. Keynesianism as

91. V. Goilo, "Burzhuaznye teorii bezrabotitsy na sluzhbe monopolii," *Voprosy Ekonomiki,* 1962, No. 10, p. 66.

92. M. G. Guttsait, *Khronicheskaya bezrabotitsa i nedogruzka predpriyatii SShA* (Moskva, 1961), pp. 116–121; I. Dvorkin, "Tekhnologicheskie teorii v burzhuaznoi politicheskoi ekonomii," *Voprosy Ekonomiki,* 1963, No. 4, pp. 107–120.

93. See chap. v for a discussion of D. I. Valentei, *Bezrabotitsa—neizbezhnyi sputnik kapitalizma.*

the chief school of bourgeois political economy in the epoch of the general crisis of capitalism.[94]

Professor Blyumin's three-volume *Critique of Bourgeois Political Economy* was published posthumously in 1962.[95] Blyumin made extensive criticisms of Keynes's theory throughout this study. Ryndina reviewed Blyumin's lengthy treatment of Keynes and approved of it,[96] noting the current relevance of Blyumin's findings:

> Many of Keynes's ideas to this very day are the basis of bourgeois interpretations of capitalist reproduction, the theoretical base of various anti-crisis programs, and are used in the theories of "democratic socialism." Therefore the thorough criticism of Keynes's theory in Blyumin's work has not lost its relevance for the present times.[97]

The Soviet writers of this period were aware of the inadequacy of the criticism of the Stalin period. Bregel wrote: "In the period of the cult of the personality there was substituted for a varied criticism of the anti-Marxist economic theories only one type of criticism of their bourgeois apologetic essence, which was clearly insufficient."[98] Bregel demanded that Soviet writers show the theoretical and practical insufficiency of these bourgeois theories. As an example he discussed the methodological faults of the Keynesian theory of full employment, which were, in his opinion, the subjective-psychological method, the many exchange equations, and the unemployment resulting from insufficient demands. He maintained: "Unfortunately these methodological vices are not shown in the majority of our textbooks."[99]

Despite Bregel's criticism, L. Alievskaya, in reviewing Khafizov's *The Criticism of the Theory of State Regulation of the Capitalist Economy* (Moscow, 1961), found that the standard of criticism

---

94. N. K. Karataev, ed., *Istoriya ekonomicheskikh uchenii* (Moskva, 1963), p. 25. See also N. A. Tsagolov, ed., *Kurs politicheskoi ekonomii*, I (Moskva, 1963), 516.

95. I. G. Blyumin, *Kritika burzhuaznoi politicheskoi ekonomii* (Moskva, 1962).

96. M. Ryndina, "Krizis sovremennoi burzhuaznoi politicheskoi ekonomii," *Voprosy Ekonomiki*, 1963, No. 6, pp. 132–140.

97. *Ibid.*, p. 135.

98. E. Bregel, "Kurs politicheskoi ekonomiki i kritika antimarksistskikh teorii," *Kommunist*, 1964, No. 8, p. 90.

99. *Ibid.*, p. 95.

had improved.[100] Alievskaya agreed with Khafizov's findings that Keynes provided the basis for the theories of the state regulation of the economy and that all these theories were concerned with investment. Her opinion of the current state of Soviet criticism was:

> R. Kh. Khafizov's book as well as other works published recently show that the level of analysis of Soviet economists of contemporary bourgeois economic theories has been raised considerably. The scientific community waits for new books from our economists that contain profound Marxist criticism of contemporary bourgeois economic theories and in particular the different varieties of the theories of "economic growth."[101]

There was indeed more varied criticism during this period. Osadchaya allowed Foster, the American Communist, his theory of the two variants of Keynesianism,[102] for which he had been taken to task earlier.[103] In other works, Osadchaya made further reference to the three basic schools of growth that she had previously identified: Keynesian, left-Keynesian, and sociological.[104] She identified Joan Robinson as a left-Keynesian. A similar estimate of Miss Robinson was given by Volkov: "Joan Robinson occupies a special place. She holds progressive views on the policy of peaceful coexistence of the two systems and the friendly relations between the capitalist and the socialist world, and in the area of theory for the past ten years she has attempted to adapt Marxism to Keynesianism."[105] However, Volkov and Osadchaya still numbered her in the ranks of the bourgeois economists.

The Soviets placed other Western economists in this category as well. Ryndina reported on a conference of Marxist economists held in Sofia in May, 1964, in which "progressive" views were recognized in the West.[106] Further, Ryndina suggested the possibility of

---

100. L. Alievskaya, "Kniga o Keinse i ego posledovatelyakh," *Mirovaya Ekonomika i Mezhdunarodnye Otnosheniya*, 1963, No. 5, pp. 146–148.
101. *Ibid.*, p. 148.
102. I. Osadchaya, "Ekonomicheskaya teoriya Keinsa," *Mirovaya Ekonomika i Mezhdunarodnye Otnosheniya*, 1958, No. 6, p. 140.
103. See chap. v.
104. Osadchaya, *Kritika*, p. 2.
105. Volkov, *Sovremennaya burzhuaznaya politicheskaya ekonomika Anglii*, p. 9.
106. M. Ryndina, "Novye tendentsii v burzhuaznoi politicheskoi ekonomii," *Voprosy Ekonomiki*, 1964, No. 9, pp. 149–153.

creating an anti-monopoly front to help these "progressives" cross over to Marxism:

In the reports it was noticed that in separate works of bourgeois economists there are found sometimes progressive tendencies . . . . We must therefore learn to recognize those economists who are not apologists of monopoly, those who begin to doubt the possibility of the preservation of capitalism. While criticizing their mistakes, it is necessary at the same time to use their theories in the interests of creating an anti-monopoly front and thus help such economists to cross over to positions of true Marxist science.[107]

Although it was proper for "progressives" to become Marxists, the Soviets would not permit any merging of Marxism with Keynesianism. Dvorkin was particularly severe in condemning all the revisionist suggestions that Marxism merge with Keynesianism and current bourgeois theories.[108] Revisionists claimed that Keynes had scientifically reconstructed political economy, but Dvorkin answered: "In reality, the Keynesian school has carried out the reconstruction of bourgeois political economy adaptable most fully to the conditions of contemporary capitalism. As a result, therefore, it has become the most widespread of the bourgeois economic schools."[109] Dvorkin predicted bankruptcy for Keynesianism and for those attempts to merge it with Marxism.

Yu. Olsevich found that many bourgeois economists were overzealous in their criticism of Marxism but had little understanding of it.[110] Further, he even accused Keynes of borrowing from Marx:

An example of this was given by none other than the spiritual father of the majority of contemporary bourgeois economists, Keynes, who once admitted that he did not possess the patience to read the works of Marx to the end. He carried to his grave the secret as to where exactly he did stop reading. We are not intending, of course, to blame Keynes for not reading the whole of Marx's works because those rational grains that are sifted from the subjective idealistic chaff have obviously been borrowed from Marxism (which, by the way, prominent Keynesians do not attempt

107. *Ibid.*, pp. 151–152.
108. I. N. Dvorkin, "O revizionistskikh teoriyakh 'sliyaniya' burzhuaznoi politicheskoi ekonomii s marksistskoi," *Voprosy Ekonomiki*, 1960, No. 8, pp. 78–88.
109. *Ibid.*, p. 85.
110. Yu. Olsevich, "Novye manevry burzhuaznykh kritikov trudovoi teorii stoimosti," *Voprosy Ekonomiki*, 1963, No. 9, pp. 103–119.

to deny). These grains were not few, and it was not for nothing that Keynes had to throw away reservation and assure his nervous class colleagues that "in any case" he and his theory were on the bourgeois side of the barricades.[111]

N. Karataev was of the opinion that the supporters of Keynesianism tried to please everyone: "The supporters of Keynes selected a sufficient quantity of quotations from his book to prove that in Keynesian teaching is found individualism, concern over the interest of the individual capitalists, and an active state policy."[112]

In the competition between the socialist and capitalist systems war was ruled out as a means for settling disputes, but the Soviets did not admit to peaceful coexistence on the ideological front and so their criticism of Keynes continued. The program of the Twenty-Second Congress of the CPSU declared: "In the contemporary world a bitter struggle goes on between the two ideologies—the communist and the bourgeois ideology. This struggle is the reflection in the spiritual life of humanity of the historical progress of the transition from capitalism to socialism."[113]

In this struggle the tasks of the economists were outlined by K. Plotnikov in an article on "Economic Science in the Contemporary Stage of Communist Construction":

Soviet scholars and economists in this accounting must put forth all their strength to justify with honor the great trust of the party, to achieve new outstanding victories in all the decisive branches of human learning, and to introduce a working contribution to the matter of the construction of communism.[114]

Although the Soviets criticized Keynes throughout this period, the manner of their criticism was varied. Even though harsh tones were still present, the criticism was more muted and restrained. An example of this lenient tone during this period was the entry on Keynes in the latest edition (fifth) of Lenin's works:

111. *Ibid.*, p. 110.
112. N. Karataev, "Burzhuaznye kontseptsii istorii ekonomicheskoi mysli," *Voprosy Ekonomiki*, 1963, No. 2, p. 104.
113. *Programma Kommunisticheskoi partii Sovetskogo Soyuza*, Prinyata XXII sezdom KPSS (Moskva, 1961), p. 51.
114. K. Plotnikov, "Ekonomicheskaya nauka na sovremennom etape kommunisticheskogo stroitelstva," *Voprosy Ekonomiki*, 1961, No. 8, p. 25.

Keynes, John Maynard (1883–1946)—English vulgar bourgeois economist, apologist of state-monopoly capitalism. From 1915 an official in the Ministry of Finance of England. In 1919 participated in the work of the Paris peace conference. Went into retirement in June 1919 and in a series of works subjected the instability of the system of the imperialist Versailles Treaty to sharp criticism. From 1921 was a representative of a large English insurance company. In the thirties was the founder of one of the apologetic schools of bourgeois political economy (called by his name "Keynesianism"), according to which the bourgeois state somehow is able to "regulate" capitalism and to "guarantee" within its framework a planned economy without crises and unemployment.[115]

This is in marked contrast to previous biographical notes on Keynes in which, it will be remembered, Lenin's own virulent attack on Keynes was customarily included.

The changing conditions noted above, together with the appearance of the trends and opinions analyzed in this chapter, helped to produce a vast increase of Soviet works on bourgeois political economy and a better perspective of Keynes on the part of the Soviets. At the height of the cold war Keynes was *the* ideologist of monopoly capitalism. More recently the Soviets have revised their estimate, and though they acknowledge the Keynesian school as dominant in the West, other schools have now been recognized. Their views showed variations and minor differences regarding Keynesianism, but these did not differ in substance from the entry on Keynes in the fifth edition of Lenin's *Complete Works* appearing in 1963. This is presumed to be the official Soviet position, and it is indeed a very different assessment from Volodin's *Keins—ideolog monopolisticheskogo kapitala* of 1953, to which, surprisingly enough, references ceased to appear during this period of peaceful coexistence.

---

115. V. I. Lenin, *Polnoe sobranie sochinenii*, 5th ed.; XLII (Moskva, 1963), 525; the same entry was also found in XLI, 585.

VIII. *Conclusion*

This study has reviewed the Soviet position with respect to Keynes from the founding of the Soviet state in 1917 to the retirement of Nikita S. Khrushchev in October, 1964. It seems appropriate to conclude with some general observations reflecting the Soviet estimate of Keynes over the entire period under review.

Keynes came to the attention of the Soviets early in their history. Lenin himself referred to Keynes on a number of occasions, and his report to the Second Congress of the Communist International on July 19, 1920, in Petrograd was based largely on Keynes's *The Economic Consequences of the Peace*. However, Lenin drew a sharp distinction between Keynes the economist and Keynes the avowed bourgeois. As an economist, Keynes received the highest compliment that Lenin could give to any representative of capitalism, that is, the correct analysis of historical trends. On the other hand, Lenin always depicted Keynes as a confirmed hater of bolshevism. In this respect Lenin made it perfectly clear to his listeners that they should keep this distinction in mind. Lenin's assessment of Keynes was not seriously challenged by Trotsky or by other Soviet leaders, though Trotsky's views showed a sharp divergence from Keynes in relation to the Malthusian problem of overpopulation. Lenin's references to Keynes were quoted by Soviet writers throughout the period under study. It appears, however, that Soviet writers found it convenient to select different passages for quotation from Lenin at different periods, according to the political climate, since some of Lenin's utterances showed Keynes in a more unfavorable light than others. At the height of the cold war, for example, Lenin's most virulent attack on Keynes was given prominence, while his many relatively favorable remarks were conveniently ignored.

The Soviets, as might be expected, were consistently interested in and critical of Keynes; a review of the literature on bourgeois politi-

cal economy revealed that no other contemporary Western economist has received as much notice. Criticism of bourgeois political
economy is a recognized activity of Soviet economists, and there
have been a number of Soviet specialists in this field. These economists have been connected with the various economic institutes of
the Academy of Sciences or with a major university. They contributed frequently to the literature and the same names appeared with
increasing regularity. Among the earlier contributors were L. B.
Alter, I. G. Blyumin, E. Ya. Bregel, I. N. Dvorkin, I. Kuzminov,
M. Ryndina, I. A. Trakhtenberg, and E. S. Varga. Some of the
later contributors were R. Khafizov, S. A. Khavina, G. Khromushin,
G. Kozlov, S. Nikitin, A. Pokrovskii, S. L. Vygodskii, P. Oldak,
Yu. Olsevich, and I. Osadchaya. They appeared well acquainted
with Keynes's works, and it was their responsibility to attack, unmask, crush, or refute Keynes according to the demands of the
situation.

The Soviets commented on Keynes's earlier publications prior to
The General Theory, and a number of them were translated into
Russian. A review of Keynes's major work, *The General Theory*,
first appeared in 1946. Although the English edition of the book
appeared in 1936, the Soviets were slow in recognizing its importance but after 1946 paid increasing attention to it. Keynes's theory
became known as Keynesianism in the Soviet Union. It was first
seen in competition with other bourgeois schools of economics, but
within a relatively short time the Soviets acknowledged Keynesianism to be the dominant bourgeois school. As a result of this development, the Russian translation of *The General Theory* appeared
in 1948.

This was the first translation of a work of Western bourgeois
economic theory to appear in Russian following World War II. An
analysis of the Russian translation revealed that it was a somewhat
expurgated edition. The translation was faithful to the text where
followed but there were several deliberate omissions, and the editorial remarks in footnotes were profuse and biased. Among the
most striking omissions were Keynes's preface, certain references
to totalitarian societies, and a long reference to the life and thought
of Silvio Gesell. The translation contained a lengthy introductory

article by Professor I. G. Blyumin, who prepared the reader for the "correct" interpretation of Keynes's theory. The translation was reviewed by V. S. Volodin, who found the effort inadequate and lacking in strong party-type criticism. Later, Volodin wrote *Keynes —the Ideologist of Monopoly Capital,* which certainly could not be accused of having this deficiency.

Certain general observations can be made in regard to the development of Soviet Keynesian criticism. The major one is that the Soviets were consistently opposed to Keynes and his theory. From Lenin to the resignation of Khrushchev, the Soviets assessed Keynes as a "bourgeois" and his theory as an apology for capitalism. In this respect, they were correct from their viewpoint, for their ideology and Keynesianism are incompatible. However, this did not prevent them from varying their criticism of Keynes in intensity and scope.

A real point-by-point rebuttal of *The General Theory* was not found in the literature, nor was there any attempt to assess Keynes's work in an objective analytical manner such as Western economists generally employ when criticizing each other. The Soviet writers simply selected certain fundamental issues and dealt at length with them. Among these were economic crises, unemployment, militarization of the economy, state intervention in the economy, real wages, and exploitation. For instance, Volodin's full-length work on Keynes was an attack on Keynes as an apologist of capitalism and on his theory as the basis for the militarization of the economy. Another important charge repeatedly and erroneously made against Keynes by a great number of Soviet economists was that his theory was inflationary even under conditions of widespread unemployment. The Soviets were presumably forced to make this point in order to conform to the Marxist tenet of the relative and absolute impoverishment of the worker in capitalist society. Much of the criticism was repetitive and boring. Frequently one writer simply echoed another on Keynes. The writers often chose the same quotations from Marx and Lenin to refute Keynes. In most respects the development of Keynesian criticism in the Soviet Union has not reached the level attained in the West.

Following World War II, the Soviets first simply considered Keynesianism another school of bourgeois political economy. They soon elevated Keynesianism to the predominant school, and *The General Theory* was translated into Russian. This was at the height of the cold war and the criticism of this period was harsh and rigid. This was the period of the Varga debate, and the Soviets refused to recognize the significance of the role of the state in the capitalist system. Since the Soviets identified Keynesianism as the school of regulated capitalism or state intervention in the economy, they were unalterably opposed to his theory. Only one interpretation of Keynesianism was allowed, and planning was not considered feasible within the capitalist system.

There was much distortion of Keynes during this Stalinist period, and he was shown in a most unfavorable light. The Soviets resorted to the most unfair and cruel type of slander in portraying Keynes in the role of a warmonger. Volodin's work on Keynes appeared during this period, and it was representative of the Soviet efforts to discredit him. Keynesian influence was uncovered everywhere. The Soviets charged that revisionists and reformist movements based their economic programs on Keynesianism, and they found its harmful influence not only dominant in Western countries such as Great Britain, the United States, France, West Germany, and Austria, but also at work in India, and even in satellite countries such as Yugoslavia and Poland.

Socialism in its Western form was no longer hailed as a sign of progress, but condemned for its alliance with Keynesianism, which the Soviets considered to be a force of international dimensions utterly hostile to the interests of their country. A frequent quotation was one of Stalin's to the effect that fascism and social democracy were really twins and not opposites.[1] Khrushchev was quoted as describing revisionism as the "Trojan horse" of imperialism.[2] These movements were accused of advocating an improved capitalism without the sharp conflicts of the class struggle. They attempted to soothe the contradictions of capitalism instead of revealing their

---

1. See, for example, A. I. Kochetkov, "Keinsianstvo—ideologiya reaksionnoi imperialisticheskoi burzhuazii," *Izvestiya Akademii Nauk SSSR*, 1950, No. 6, p. 437. The reference was Stalin, *Sochinenie*, p. 282.

2. Dvorkin, *Kritika*, p. 9. Dvorkin referred to Khrushchev's speech to the Seventh Congress of the Communist party of Bulgaria.

sharpness. Keynesianism, in the opinion of the Soviets, had provided the current theoretical basis for these policies. The Soviets constantly noted the fight of the "progressives" in the West in their struggle against these movements and Keynesianism.

The Khrushchev period of peaceful coexistence brought changes in the Soviet treatment of Keynesianism. Slowly at first but steadily the criticism became less rigid, and toward the end of this period it can be viewed as sophisticated when compared with that of the Stalinist period. References to Stalin's views on bourgeois economics and to Volodin's work started to fade away. Translations of other bourgeois economists such as Hansen, Harrod, and Haberler appeared in Russian. Russian works began to contain better referencing, indexes, and bibliographies. Soviet economists condemned the rigid one-viewpoint approach found during the period of the cult of the personality. There was a demand to produce better and more varied criticism of bourgeois economic theories.

This attitude produced certain results. The Soviets now recognized the various schools of political economy existing in the West. The role of the state was acknowledged, and planning of certain sectors was now admitted to be possible in the capitalist system. The Soviets noticed the various kinds of Keynesianism and dealt with the differences among them. They began to distinguish between orthodox Keynesians, neo-Keynesians, left-wing Keynesians, and radical Keynesians. These brands all had in common, however, the theory of regulation of the economy, or state intervention. Keynesianism was still regarded as the dominant school in this respect, but the Soviets found that it was challenged by other schools, notably by the neo-liberals and the economic conservatives. They acknowledged the Keynesian influence on other schools, especially on the growth, macroeconomics, dynamics, and econometric schools. Also, instead of quoting only Western communist critics of Keynes, such as Victor Perlo, William Z. Foster, and Anna Rochester, the Soviets now made reference to reputable Western economists who were critical of his theories. Keynes now appeared in Soviet textbooks for university courses in political economy and economic thought.

The Soviets appeared to make a more realistic appraisal of the West during this period and were forced to account for the fact that the capitalist system was still healthy and even buoyant. The dire predictions of crisis and collapse seemed inappropriate. The "general crisis of capitalism" had continued since World War I, so the Soviets designated a third stage in this crisis in 1960. Keynesianism was found to be the answer of the capitalist system during the first and second stages of the general crisis. In the opinion of the Soviets, the success of the socialist system had forced the capitalist system to respond with theories of growth and dynamics. The Soviets found that these theories were based on and were an outgrowth of Keynesianism.

That Soviet criticism was broader in scope and less intense than in the Stalinist period did not signify any official acceptance of bourgeois political economic theory. In the battle of the two systems, there was no cease-fire in the ideological struggle. Certain Western "progressives" were accepted in an anti-monopoly front, but all suggestions of any combining or merging of Keynesianism with Marxism received not the slightest consideration from the Soviets. In their opinion, Marx and Keynes were still incompatible. In this respect, the Veritas Foundation, which published *Keynes at Harvard*, belies its name by the unfounded and untruthful allegation that Keynesianism "is not economics. It is left-wing political theory."[3]
In point of fact, the Soviets have condemned Keynes throughout the period under review.

The Soviets have constantly predicted the collapse of capitalism, holding it to be in a state of general crisis, and forecasting its doom after World War I, during the great depression, and following World War II. The so-called general crisis of capitalism still continues. This crisis covers so lengthy a period that the Soviets have conveniently divided it into stages. There are no longer predictions of immediate collapse. Instead, we have opinions like that of Varga, the doyen of Soviet economists specializing in capitalism:

The exceedingly complicated conditions of the historical transition from capitalism to socialism do not permit a more concrete forecast. However, one can predict with virtual certainty that the twentieth century is the last century of the existence of capitalism. At the end of this

3. Veritas Foundation, *Keynes at Harvard* (New York, 1960), p. 2.

century capitalism generally will not exist or will only remain in insignificant forms.[4]

How insignificant these forms will appear to Soviet economists writing thirty years hence is an interesting point for speculation. In the meantime the capitalist system continues to survive. Since the Soviets have referred to Keynes as the so-called savior, doctor, restorer, high priest, and messiah of capitalism and to *The General Theory* as the "Bible" of monopoly capitalism, from the Soviet viewpoint it follows that Keynes has played a considerable and significant role in prolonging its existence.

4. E. Varga, *Kapitalizm dvadtsatogo veka* (Moskva, 1961), p. 147.

Bibliography of works cited: Index

Translation of titles of Soviet periodicals

Finansy SSSR—Finances of the USSR
Izvestiya Akademii Nauk SSSR—Bulletin of the Academy of Sciences of the USSR
Izvestiya Akademii Nauk Turkmenskoi SSR—Bulletin of the Academy of Sciences of the Turkmenistan SSR
Kommunist Estonii—Communist of Estonia
Kommunist Sovetskoi Latvii—Communist of Soviet Latvia
Kommunist Ukrainy—Communist of the Ukraine
Kommunist Uzbekistana—Communist of Uzbekistan
Mirovaya Ekonomika i Mezhdunarodnye Otnosheniya—World Economy and International Relations
Mirovoe Khozyaistvo i Mirovaya Politika—World Economy and World Politics
Nauchnye Doklady Vysshei Shkoly—Scientific Reports of Higher Schools
Novyi Mir—New World
Problemy Ekonomiki—Problems of Economics
Planovoe Khozyaistvo—Planned Economy
Sovetskie Finansy—Soviet Finances
Sotsialisticheskii Trud—Socialist Labor
Sovremennyi Vostok—Contemporary East
Vestnik Moskovskogo Universiteta—Herald of Moscow University
Voprosy Ekonomiki—Questions of Economics

Bibliography of works cited

Sources in the Russian language

Books, monographs, and pamphlets

Akademiya Nauk SSSR. *Reformizm, revisionizm i problemy sovremennogo kapitalizma.* Moskva, 1959.

Alter, L. B. *Burzhuaznaya politicheskaya ekonomiya SShA.* Moskva, 1961.

———. *Krushenie teorii "planovogo kapitalizma."* Moskva, 1954.

Arzumanyan, A. A. *Novyi etap obshchego krizisa kapitalizma.* Moskva, 1961.

Belyaeva, Z. N., and V. A. Budarin. *Kritika sovremennykh burzhuaznykh reformistskikh i revizionistskikh ekonomicheskikh teorii.* Moskva, 1962.

Blyumin, I. G. *Istoriya ekonomicheskikh uchenii.* Moskva, 1961.

———. *Kritika burzhuaznoi politicheskoi ekonomii.* 3 vols. Moskva, 1962.

———. *Kritika sovremennoi burzhuaznoi politicheskoi ekonomii Anglii.* Moskva, 1953.

———, ed. *Kritika teorii reguliruemogo kapitalizma.* Moskva, 1959.

———. *Ocherki sovremennoi burzhuaznoi politicheskoi ekonomii SShA.* Moskva, 1956.

———. *Ocherki sovremennoi politicheskoi ekonomii.* Moskva, 1956.

———. *O sovremennoi burzhuaznoi politicheskoi ekonomii.* Moskva, 1958.

Blyumin, I. G., and I. N. Dvorkin, *Mif o narodnom kapitalizme.* Moskva, 1957.

Bolshaya Sovetskaya Entsiklopediya. 1st ed. 65 vols. Moskva, 1926–1947.

Bolshaya Sovetskaya Entsiklopediya. 2nd ed. 51 vols. Moskva, 1949–1958.

Bregel, E. Ya., ed. *Monopolisticheskii kapitalizm-imperializm.* Moskva, 1961.

Bunkina, M. K. *Kritika pravosotsialisticheskoi teorii "vrastaniya" kapitalizma v sotsialism.* Moskva, 1961.

Dolukin, V. I., and V. P. Trepelkov. *Obshchii krizis kapitalizma.* Moskva, 1963.

Dvorkin, I. N. *Ideologiya politiki pravykh leiboristov na sluzhbe monopolii.* Moskva, 1953.

———. *Kritika ekonomicheskikh teorii pravykh sotsialistov, Zapadnogermanskikh i Avstriiskikh.* Moskva, 1959.

———. *Tekhnicheskii progress i burzhuaznaya politekonomiya.* Moskva, 1961.

Eventov, L. Ya. *Voennaya ekonomika Anglii.* Moskva, 1946.

Glukharev, L. I. *O sovremennom gosudarstvenno-monopolisticheskom kapitalizme.* Moskva, 1963.

Guttsait, M. G. *Khronicheskaya bezrabotitsa i nedogruzka predpriyatii SShA.* Moskva, 1961.

Iton, Dzh. *Marks protiv Keinsa.* Translated by M. A. Menshikova. Moskva, 1958.

Karataev, N. K., ed. *Istoriya ekonomicheskikh uchenii.* Moskva, 1963.

Keins, Dzh. M. *Obshchaya teoriya zanyatosti, protsenta i deneg.* Translated by N. N. Lyubimov. Introductory article by I. G. Blyumin. Moskva, 1948.

Khafizov, R. Kh. *Kritika teorii gosudarstvennogo regulirovaniya kapitalisticheskoi ekonomiki.* Moskva, 1961.

Khavina, S. A. *Protiv burzhuaznykh ekonomicheskikh psevdoteorii sotsializma.* Moskva, 1962.

Khrushchev, N. S. *O revolyutsionnom rabochem i kommunisticheskom dvizhenii.* Moskva, 1963.

Kozlov, G. A., and S. P. Pervushin, eds. *Kratkii ekonomicheskii slovar.* Moskva, 1958.

Lenin, V. I. *Polnoe sobranie sochinenii.* 5th ed. 55 vols. Moskva, 1958–19—.

———. *Sochineniya.* 4th ed. 35 vols. Moskva, 1941–1950.

Leninskii sbornik. 3rd ed. 35 vols. Moskva, 1925–1945.

Lyubimov, N. N. *Mezhdunarodnyi kapitalisticheskii kredit—orudie imperialisticheskoi agressii.* Moskva, 1951.

Mamalui, A. P., ed. *Kritika sovremennykh burzhuaznykh reformistskikh i revizionistskikh teorii po voprosam politicheskoi ekonomii.* Kharkov, 1963.

Nikitin, S. M. *Kritika ekonomicheskoi teorii "planirovaniya" kapitalisticheskoi ekonomiki.* Moskva, 1962.

Osadchaya, I. M. *Kritika sovremennykh burzhuaznykh teorii ekonomicheskogo rosta.* Moskva, 1963.

Pokrovskii, A. I. *Frantsuzskaya burzhuaznaya politicheskaya ekonomiya.* Moskva, 1961.

Polyanskii, F. Ya., ed. *Istoki sovremennogo revizionizma i ego burzhuaznaya sushchnost.* Moskva, 1961.

Programma Kommunisticheskoi partii Sovetskogo Soyuza. Prinyata XXII sezdom KPSS. Moskva, 1961.

Ryndina, M. N. *Burzhuaznye ekonomisty Anglii i SShA na sluzhbe imperialisticheskoi reaktsii.* Moskva, 1954.

————, ed. *Kritika burzhuaznoi ekonomicheskoi teorii.* Moskva, 1960.

————. *Kritika ekonomicheskikh teorii revizionistov.* Moskva, 1960.

Smit, M. N. *Ocherki istorii burzhuaznoi politicheskoi ekonomii.* Moskva, 1961.

Solyus, G. P. *Razvitie gosudarstvenno—monopolisticheskogo kapitalizma v usloviyakh obshchego krizisa kapitalizma.* Moskva, 1963.

Stalin, I. V. *Ekonomicheskie problemy sotsializma v SSSR.* Moskva, 1952.

Struve, G. P., and T. S. Lure. *Ekonomicheskie posledstiya mira.* Stockholm, 1921.

Tarle, E. V. *Europa v epokhu imperializma.* Moskva, 1927.

Trakhtenberg, I. A. *Finansovye itogi voiny.* Moskva, 1946.

————. *Kapitalisticheskoe vosproizvodstvo i ekonomicheskie krizisy.* Leningrad, 1947.

————. *Kapitalisticheskoe vosproizvodstvo i ekonomicheskie krizisy.* 2nd ed. rev. Moskva, 1954.

Trotskii, L. *Kuda idyot Angliya?* Moskva, 1925.

————. *Pyat let kominterna.* Moskva, 1924.

————. *Sochineniya.* 21 vols. Moskva, 1925–1927.

Tsagolov, N. A., ed. *Kritika sovremennykh burzhuaznykh reformistskikh i revizionistskikh ekonomicheskikh teorii.* Moskva, 1960.

————, ed. *Kurs politicheskoi ekonomii.* 2 vols. Moskva, 1963.

Valentei, D. I. *Bezrabotitsa—neizbezhnyi sputnik kapitalizma.* Moskva, 1951.

Varga, E. S. *Izmeneniya v ekonomike kapitalizma v itoge vtoroi mirovoi voiny.* Moskva, 1946.

————. *Kapitalizm dvadtsatogo veka.* Moskva, 1961.

————, ed. *Mirovoe khozyaistvo v 1936g.* Moskva, 1937.

————. *Osnovnye voprosy ekonomiki i politiki imperializma.* Moskva, 1953.

————. *Sovremennyi kapitalizm i ekonomicheskie krizisy.* Moskva, 1963.

Volkov, M. Ya. *Sovremennaya burzhuazhnaya politicheskaya ekonomiya Anglii.* Moskva, 1963.
Volodin, V. S. *Keins—ideolog monopolisticheskogo kapitala.* Moskva, 1953.
Vygodskii, S. L. *Ocherki teorii sovremennogo kapitalizma.* Moskva, 1961.

Journals and newspapers

Aizenshadt, A. "Uchonye prisluzhniki amerikanskogo kapitala," *Planovoe Khozyaistvo*, 1947, No. 4, pp. 80–89.
Aleksandrovskii, A. "Krizis burzhuaznoi ekonomicheskoi mysli vo Frantsii," *Voprosy Ekonomiki*, 1957, No. 3, pp. 80–92.
Alievskaya, L. "Kniga o Keinse i ego posledovatelyakh," *Mirovaya Ekonomika i Mezhdunarodnye Otnosheniya*, 1963, No. 5, pp. 146–148.
Alter, L. B. "Burzhuaznaya politicheskaya ekonomika—orudie podzhigatelei voiny," *Planovoe Khozyaistvo*, 1950, No. 4, pp. 63–80.
―――. "O noveishei burzhuaznoi teorii ekonomicheskogo rosta," *Voprosy Ekonomiki*, 1961, No. 6, 84–98.
―――. "Teoreticheskie oruzhenostsy amerikanskogo imperializma," *Planovoe Khozyaistvo*, 1947, No. 5, pp. 74–94.
―――. "Teoriya i praktika kapitalisticheskogo regulirovaniya," *Mirovaya Ekonomika i Mezhdunarodnye Otnosheniya*, 1964, No. 3, pp. 63–72.
Arutinyan, A. "Garvardskie ekonomisty i burzhuaznoe konyunkturovedenie," *Problemy Ekonomiki*, 1940, No. 9, pp. 151–165.
Atlas, Z. Review of S. Vygodskii, *Kredit i kreditnaya politika v SShA* (Moskva, 1936), *Planovoe Khozyaistvo*, 1937, No. 2, pp. 172–175.
Berri, L. "O 'planirovanii' na kapitalisticheskom predpriyatii," *Voprosy Ekonomiki*, 1949, No. 8, pp. 79–80.
Blyumin, I. G. "Amerikanskie ekonomisty na sluzhbe monopolii," *Voprosy Ekonomiki*, 1948, No. 8, pp. 52–65.
―――. "Burzhuaznye ekonomisty na sluzhbe militarizma i voiny," *Voprosy Ekonomiki*, 1952, No. 9, pp. 107–119.
―――. "Ekonomicheskoe uchenie Keinsa," *Izvestiya Akademii Nauk SSSR*, Otdelenie ekonomiki i prava, 1946, No. 4, pp. 301–319.
―――. "Keinsianstvo na sluzhbe imperialisticheskoi reaktsii," *Voprosy Ekonomiki*, 1952, No. 2, pp. 123–126.
―――. "Keins—prorok reguliruemogo kapitalizma," *Vestnik Moskovskogo Universiteta*, 1947, No. 4, pp. 43–66.

————. "O krizise sovremennoi burzhuaznoi politicheskoi ekonomii," *Voprosy Ekonomiki*, 1957, No. 12, pp. 64–75.

————. "Londonskaya shkola v politicheskoi ekonomii," *Izvestiya Akademii Nauk SSSR*, Otdelenie ekonomiki i prava, 1946, No. 3, pp. 217–230.

————. "Review of Erich Roll, *A History of Economic Thought*" (London, 1938), *Problemy Ekonomiki*, 1939, No. 5, pp. 203–206.

————. "Sotsialno-ekonomicheskie vozzreniya Gobsona," *Izvestiya Akademii Nauk SSSR*, Otdelenie ekonomiki i prava, 1947, No. 4, pp. 265–277.

Blyumin, I. G., and I. Dvorkin. "O sovremennoi politicheskoi ekonomii promezhutochnykh klassov," *Voprosy Ekonomiki*, 1955, No. 9, pp. 148–162.

Bogachevskii, M. "Burzhuaznaya apologetika pod vidom 'noveishei teorii' gosudarstvennogo kredita," *Finansy SSSR*, 1963, No. 7, pp. 43–52.

Bogdanov, O. "Zoloto v finansovoi sisteme imperializma," *Mirovaya Ekonomika i Mezhdunarodnye Otnosheniya*, 1963, No. 8, pp. 63–72.

Bregel, E. "Burzhuaznye i revizionistkie teorii 'smeshannoi ekonomiki,' " *Voprosy Ekonomiki*, 1948, No. 8, pp. 66–80.

————. "Kurs politicheskoi ekonomiki i kritika antimarksistskikh teorii," *Kommunist*, 1964, No. 8, pp. 90–97.

————. "Rost nalogovogo bremeni i inflyatsiya v kapitalisticheskikh stranakh," *Voprosy Ekonomiki*, 1953, No. 2, pp. 75–91.

————. "Sovremennye burzhuaznye i reformistskie teorii inflyatsii," *Voprosy Ekonomiki*, 1959, No. 4, pp. 91–105.

————. "Sovremennye burzhuaznye teorii bezrabotitsy," *Mirovaya Ekonomika i Mezhdunarodnye Otnosheniya*, 1958, No. 7, pp. 78–93.

Cheprakov, V. "Burzhuaznye ekonomisty i gosudarstvenno-monopolisticheskii kapitalizm," *Voprosy Ekonomiki*, 1955, No. 9, pp. 134–147.

————. "Burzhuaznye ekonomisty SShA—apologety imperialisticheskoi reaktsii i agressii," *Bolshevik*, 1952, No. 24, pp. 93–107.

————. "Gosudarstvenno-monopolisticheskii kapitalizm i burzhuaznaya politicheskaya ekonomiya," *Voprosy Ekonomiki*, 1962, No. 7, pp. 83–98.

————. "Sovremennyi kapitalizm i antimarksizm," *Kommunist*, 1957, No. 17, pp. 65–82.

Chermenskii, V. "Obnishchanie trudyashchikhsya v kapitalisticheskikh stranakh," *Planovoe Khozyaistvo*, 1950, No. 2, pp. 73–90.

Dalin, S. "Ekonomicheskaya teoriya amerikanskogo rente," *Mirovaya Ekonomika i Mezhdunarodnye Otnosheniya*, 1964, No. 10, pp. 61–75.

————. "Prodolzhenie legendy," *Mirovaya Ekonomika i Mezhdunarodnye Otnosheniya*, 1963, No. 8, pp. 142–145.

"Diskussiya po knige E. Varga," *Mirovoe Khozyaistvo i Mirovaya Politika*, 1947, No. 11, pp. 1–64.

Dmitriev, N. "Progressivnye ekonomisty SShA v borbe protiv ideologii militarizma i reaktsii," *Voprosy Ekonomiki*, 1955, No. 2, pp. 70–82.

Dvorkin, I. N. "Ekonomicheskoe sorevnovanie dvykh sistem i sovremennaya burzhuaznaya politicheskaya ekonomiya," *Voprosy Ekonomiki*, 1964, No. 10, pp. 99–110.

————. "Leiborizm—ideinaya opora imperializma," *Voprosy Ekonomiki*, 1949, No. 5, pp. 61–82.

————. "Pravoleiboristskii variant teorii neo-kapitalizma," *Mirovaya Ekonomika i Mezhdunarodnye Otnosheniya*, 1963, No. 6, pp. 144–148.

————. "Reaktsionnaya sushchnost sovremennogo reformizma," *Voprosy Ekonomiki*, 1957, No. 6, pp. 85–96.

————. "O revizionistskikh teoriyakh 'sliyaniya' burzhuaznoi politicheskoi ekonomii s marksistskoi," *Voprosy Ekonomiki*, 1960, No. 8, pp. 78–88.

————. "Tekhnologicheskie teorii v burzhuaznoi politicheskoi ekonomike," *Voprosy Ekonomiki*, 1963, No. 4, pp. 107–120.

Eidelnant, A. "Rasstroistvo kapitalisticheskikh denezhnykh sistem v period obshchego krizisa kapitalizma," *Voprosy Ekonomiki*, 1953, No. 7, pp. 36–47.

Entov, R. "Sovremennye keinsianskie teorii defitsitnogo finansirovaniya i mif o 'demokratizatsii gosudarstvennogo dolga,' " *Voprosy Ekonomiki*, 1960, No. 10, pp. 54–64.

Epshtein, S. "Keins—vdokhnovitel opportunizma," *Novyi Mir*, 1959, No. 1, pp. 265–267.

F., L. Review of John M. Keynes, *How to Pay for the War* (London, 1940), *Problemy Ekonomiki*, 1940, No. 9, pp. 172–173.

Freiman, L. "Bezrabotitsa v kapitalisticheskikh stranakh," *Planovoe Khozyaistvo*, 1938, No. 8, pp. 106–120.

Gatovskii, L. "V plenu burzhuaznoi metodologii," *Bolshevik*, 1948, No. 5, pp. 74–80.

Geller, L. "Rabochii klass kapitalisticheskikh stran posle pyat mesyatsev voiny v Evrope," *Mirovoe Khozyaistvo i Mirovaya Politika*, 1940, No. 1, pp. 61–80.

Gladkov, I. "Zashchita kapitalizma pod maskoi 'demokraticheskogo sotsializma,' " *Voprosy Ekonomiki*, 1958, No. 1, pp. 66–78.

Goilo, V. "Burzhuaznye teorii bezrabotitsy na sluzhbe monopolii," *Voprosy Ekonomiki*, 1962, No. 10, pp. 66–74.

Goldin, S. Review of Jurgen Kuczynski, *New Fashions in Wage Theory* (London, 1937), *Planovoe Khozyaistvo*, 1938, No. 12, pp. 182–184.

Grachev, F. "Burzhuaznye 'teorii' natsionalnogo dokhoda na sluzhbe imperializma," *Voprosy Ekonomiki*, 1953, No. 4, pp. 50–60.

Grigorev, A. "Voina i mobilizatsiya v stranakh kapitala," *Planovoe Khozyaistvo*, 1941, No. 1, pp. 64–78.

Gusakov, A. Review of F. I. Mikhalevskii, *Zoloto v period mirovykh voin* (Moskva, 1945), *Izvestiya Akademii Nauk SSSR*, Otdelenie ekonomiki i prava, 1946, No. 2, pp. 169–174.

Kachura, B. S. "Keinsianskaya teoriya o 'reguliruemoi ekonomike'— otkrytyi prizyv k militarizatsii," *Kommunist Uzbekistana*, 1960, No. 10.

————. "K voprosu o keinsianskikh teoriyakh stimuliruyushchego vliyaniya inflyatsii na promyshlennoe proizvodstvo SShA," *Izvestiya Akademii Nauk Turkmenskoi SSR*, Seriya obshchestvennykh nauk, 1950, No. 6, pp. 37–49.

————. "Vozmozhno li gosudarstvennoe regulirovanie khozyaistva v usloviyakh kapitalizma?" *Kommunist Ukrainy*, 1957, No. 8, pp. 62–70.

Karataev, N. "Burzhuaznye kontseptsii istorii ekonomicheskoi mysli," *Voprosy Ekonomiki*, 1963, No. 2, pp. 93–104.

Khafizov, R. "Mif o 'reguliruemoi ekonomike' kapitalizma i neizbezhnost ekonomicheskikh krizisov," *Voprosy Ekonomiki*, 1957, No. 6, pp. 114–120.

Khromushin, G. "Angliiskie leiboristy segodnya," *Nauchnye Doklady Vysshei Shkoly*, Ekonomicheskie nauki, 1959, No. 1, pp. 177–186.

————. "Antikommunizm—glavnoe soderzhanie ideologii imperializma," *Voprosy Ekonomiki*, 1963, No. 8, pp. 43–52.

Kochetkov, A. I. "Keinsianstvo—ideologiya reaktsionnoi imperialisticheskoi burzhuazii," *Izvestiya Akademii Nauk SSSR*, Otdelenie ekonomiki i prava, 1950, No. 6, pp. 425–439.

Kolganov, M. V. "O merkantilizme i neomerkantilizme v burzhuaznoi politicheskoi ekonomii," *Izvestiya Akademii Nauk SSSR*, Otdelenie ekonomiki i prava, 1947, No. 6, pp. 411–428.

Kornienko, A. "Reaktsionnaya sushchnost teorii 'reguliruemoi ekonomiki' kapitalizma," *Voprosy Ekonomiki*, 1954, No. 9, pp. 106–118.

Kotov, V. "Neoliberalnoye napravleniye v sovremennoi burzhuaznoi politekonomii," *Voprosy Ekonomiki*, 1961, No. 4, pp. 45–58.

Kozlov, G. "Torzhestvo teorii nauchnogo kommunizma," *Voprosy Ekonomiki*, 1958, No. 5, pp. 9–19.

"Kritika knigi Keinsa *Obshchaya teoriya zanyatosti, protsenta i deneg*," *Izvestiya Akademii Nauk SSSR*, Otdelenie ekonomiki i prava, 1950, No. 1, pp. 52–57.

Kuzminov, I. "Ekonomika nishchety i 'politika izobiliya,' " *Bolshevik*, 1946, No. 7–8, pp. 76–88.

———. "Ekonomika nishchety v 'vek izobiliya,' " *Bolshevik*, 1946, No. 5, pp. 60–73.

———. "O gosudarstvenno-monopolisticheskom kapitalizme," *Bolshevik*, 1948, No. 5, pp. 54–73.

———. "Keins—ideolog imperialisticheskoi reaktsii i voiny," *Bolshevik*, 1951, No. 19, pp. 39–52.

Kuznetsov, A. "Teoriya pribavochnoi stoimosti—kraeugolnyi kamen ekonomicheskogo ucheniya Marksa," *Kommunist*, 1954, No. 10, pp. 84–101.

Lang, S. "Ekonomicheskoe polozhenie Anglii," *Mirovoe Khozyaistvo i Mirovaya Politika*, 1941, No. 5, pp. 14–26.

Lemin, I. "Ideologiya i politika leiborizma na sluzhbe imperialisticheskoi reaktsii," *Bolshevik*, 1948, No. 6, pp. 43–62.

———. "Pobeda leiboristskoi partii na parlamentskikh vyborakh v Anglii," *Bolshevik*, 1945, No. 15, pp. 43–62.

Lobov-Sharonov, A. "Kritika burzhuaznoi sushchnosti leiborizma," *Sotsialisticheskii Trud*, 1959, No. 2, pp. 154–158.

Lyubimov, N. "Nekotorye problemy ekonomicheskoi teorii Keinsa," *Sovetskie Finansy*, 1947, No. 5, pp. 42–48.

Marinin, M. "Pravye leiboristy—prisluzhniki anglo-amerikanskogo imperializma," *Bolshevik*, 1951, No. 10, pp. 58–73.

———. "Pravye sotsialisty prisluzhniki imperialistov," *Bolshevik*, 1952, No. 7, pp. 73–80.

Markelev, I. "Boevoe oruzhie v borbe protiv revizionizma," *Voprosy Ekonomiki*, 1958, No. 12, pp. 139–140.

Maslov, P. P. Review of V. S. Nemchinov, *Selskhozyaistvennaya statistika s osnovami obshchei teorii* (Moskva, 1945), *Izvestiya Akademii*

Nauk SSSR, Otdelenie ekonomiki i prava, 1946, No. 3, pp. 261–264.

Mikhailov, R. "Kniga o sovremennoi burzhuaznoi politicheskoi ekonomii," *Mirovaya Ekonomika i Mezhdunarodnye Otnosheniya,* 1964, No. 9, pp. 141–145.

Miroshnikov, A. "Reaktsionaya sushchnost keinsianskoi teorii 'chrezmernykh' ili 'neklassicheskikh' sberezhenii," *Nauchnye Doklady Vysshei Shkoly, Ekonomicheskie nauki,* 1958, No. 2, pp. 88–102.

Mityurev, I. "Teoriya polnoi zanyatosti i deistvitelnost," *Mirovaya Ekonomika i Mezhdunarodnye Otnosheniya,* 1960, No. 11, pp. 76–84.

Mkrtchyan, B. " 'Levye' manipulyatsii burzhuaznykh ekonomistov," *Kommunist Estonii,* 1961, No. 4, pp. 75–83.

Momdzhyan, Kh. "Dalneishii sdvig vpravo v ideologii sovremennogo reformizma," *Kommunist,* 1960, No. 3, pp. 84–99.

Motylev, V. "Sovremennyi kapitalizm v krivom zerkale reformistskoi teorii Dzhona Strechi," *Nauchnye Doklady Vysshei Shkoly,* Ekonomicheskie nauki, 1962, No. 4, pp. 54–65.

Movshovich, G. M. "Pervyi poslevoennyi sezd amerikanskikh ekonomistov," *Izvestiya Akademii Nauk SSSR,* Otdelenie ekonomiki i prava, 1947, No. 3, pp. 190–200.

Mukin, E. "Keinsianstvo i ego reaktsionnaya sushchnost," *Kommunist Sovetskoi Latvii,* 1957, No. 5, pp. 69–74.

Myznikov, M. "Izvrashcheniya Marksizma-Leninizma v rabotakh akademika E. Varga," *Planovoe Khozyaistvo,* 1948, No. 6, pp. 69–88.

Naimov, I. "K kritike sovremennoi burzhuaznoi politekonomii," *Mirovaya Ekonomika i Mezhdunarodnye Otnosheniya,* 1964, No. 8, pp. 140–144.

"Obsuzhdenie lektsii prof. G. Myrdalya 'teoriya stoimosti Rikardo,' " *Voprosy Ekonomiki,* 1957, No. 6, pp. 152–160.

Oldak, P. "Keinsianstvo—teoreticheskaya osnova sovremennogo opportunizma," *Mirovaya Ekonomika i Mezhdunarodnye Otnosheniya,* 1958, No. 12, pp. 129–131.

———. "K kritike sovremennoi keinsianskoi kontseptsii ekonomicheskogo tsikla," *Mirovaya Ekonomika i Mezhdunarodnye Otnosheniya,* 1960, No. 3, pp. 128–141.

Olsevich, Yu. "Kapitalisticheskoe vosproizvodstvo i militarizatsiya ekonomiki," *Voprosy Ekonomiki,* 1962, No. 2, pp. 82–93.

———. "Novye manevry burzhuaznykh kritikov trudovoi teorii stoimosti," *Voprosy Ekonomiki,* 1963, No. 9, pp. 103–119.

Osadchaya, I. "Ekonomicheskaya teoriya Keinsa," *Mirovaya Ekonomika i Mezhdunarodnye Otnosheniya*, 1958, No. 6, pp. 138–140.

———. "Po povody sovremennykh burzhuaznykh teorii ekonomicheskoi dinamiki," *Voprosy Ekonomiki*, 1958, No. 10, pp. 91–102.

Pletnev, E. "Progressivnaya ekonomicheskaya mysl Frantsii v borbe protiv reaktsionnoi ideologii i politiki," *Voprosy Ekonomiki*, 1955, No. 6, pp. 107–120.

Plotnikov, K. "Ekonomicheskaya nauka na sovremennom etape kommunisticheskogo stroitelstva," *Voprosy Ekonomiki*, 1961, No. 8, pp. 3–25.

Pokrovskii, A. "Sudba keinsianstva vo Frantsii," *Mirovaya Ekonomika i Mezhdunarodnye Otnosheniya*, 1959, No. 9, pp. 76–85.

Polyak, P. "Ekonomicheskii krizis v Anglii," *Planovoe Khozyaistvo*, 1938, No. 9, pp. 129–142.

Polyanskii, F. "Kritika burzhuaznykh, reformistskikh i revizionistskikh teorii," *Voprosy Ekonomiki*, 1960, No. 9, pp. 102–107.

Pravda, December 6, 1960.

Pustovalov, I. "Sovremennaya burzhuaznaya politekonomiya na sluzhbe monopolisticheskogo kapitala," *Voprosy Ekonomiki*, 1963, No. 5, pp. 50–61.

Rubinshtein, A. "Chto skryvaetsya za reformistskimi 'teoriyami' vtoroi promyshlennoi revolutsii," *Voprosy Ekonomiki*, 1957, No. 12, pp. 76–89.

Rubinshtein, M. "Razoblachenie Leninym burzhuaznoi ekonomicheskoi nauki," *Voprosy Ekonomiki*, 1950, No. 4, pp. 19–36.

Russkikh, A. "Krizis burzhuaznoi ekonomicheskoi mysli sovremennoi Frantsii," *Voprosy Ekonomiki*, 1962, No. 3, pp. 136–139.

Ryndina, M. "Antinauchnaya metodologiya sovremennoi burzhuaznoi politicheskoi ekonomii," *Voprosy Ekonomiki*, 1963, No. 10, pp. 74–87.

———. "Krizis sovremennoi burzhuaznoi politicheskoi ekonomii," *Voprosy Ekonomiki*, 1963, No. 6, pp. 132–140.

———. "Novye tendentsii v burzhuaznoi politicheskoi ekonomii," *Voprosy Ekonomiki*, 1964, No. 9, pp. 149–153.

Seregin, V. "Monopolisticheskii kapital SShA—podzhigatel voiny," *Bolshevik*, 1950, No. 4, pp. 73–80.

Shapiro, A. "Plan Marshalla, razgul militarizma i ekonomicheskii krizis v SShA," *Voprosy Ekonomiki*, 1950, No. 8, pp. 125–131.

———. "Rost bezrabotitsy v kapitalisticheskikh stranakh v poslevoennyi period," *Voprosy Ekonomiki*, 1949, No. 9, pp. 76–91.

Shepilov, D. "Oruzhenostsy amerikanskogo imperializma," *Bolshevik*, 1949, No. 18, pp. 54–72.

Shundeev, V. "Ob ekonomicheskoi politike Kennedi," *Mirovaya Ekonomika i Mezhdunarodnye Otnosheniya*, 1963, No. 6, pp. 58–69.

Smit, M. "V poiskakh bezkrizisnogo kapitalizma," *Planovoe Khozyaistvo*, 1946, No. 6, pp. 75–89.

Sosenskii, I. Review of Academy of Political Science, *The Effect of the War on America's Idle Men and Money* (New York, 1940), *Mirovoe Khozyaistvo i Mirovaya Politika*, 1940, No. 10, pp. 134–135.

Trakhtenberg, I. A. "Antinauchnye domysly uchenykh lakeev monopolisticheskogo kapitala," *Bolshevik*, 1952, No. 15, pp. 74–80.

———. "Inflyatsiya i protsess kapitalisticheskogo vosproizvodstva," *Voprosy Ekonomiki*, 1954, No. 3, pp. 86–98.

———. "Mezhdunarodnyi valyutnyi fond i bank dlya rekonstrukstii i razvitiya," *Planovoe Khozyaistvo*, 1944, No. 2, pp. 69–80.

———. "Perekhod kapitalisticheskikh stran ot voennoi k mirnoi ekonomike," *Mirovoe Khozyaistvo i Mirovaya Politika*, 1946, Nos. 4–5, pp. 1–32.

———. "Proekty mezhdunarodnykh valyutnykh soglashenii," *Mirovoe Khozyaistvo i Mirovaya Politika*, 1944, No. 1–2, pp. 25–40.

Ulyanovskii, R. "Keinsianstvo ili opyt sotsialisticheskikh gosudarstv?" *Sovremennyi Vostok*, 1960, No. 7, pp. 27–29.

Varga, E. S. "Ekonomicheskii krizis v SShA predvestnik novogo mirovogo ekonomicheskogo krizisa," *Mirovoe Khozyaistvo i Mirovaya Politika*, 1938, No. 1, pp. 10–24.

———. "Konets zolotogo bloka i valyutnaya problema v period obshchego krizisa," *Mirovoe Khozyaistvo i Mirovaya Politika*, 1936, No. 11, pp. 17–30.

———. "Lzheprorok Keins," *Mirovoe Khozyaistvo i Mirovaya Politika*, 1947, No. 7, pp. 92–94.

———. Review of John M. Keynes, *How to Pay for the War* (London, 1940), *Mirovoe Khozyaistvo i Mirovaya Politika*, 1940, No. 6, pp. 200–202.

Vishnev, S. "Gosudarstvennye reservy v kapitalisticheskikh stranakh," *Planovoe Khozyaistvo*, 1940, No. 10, pp. 84–94.

Volodin, V. "Lzheteoriya Keinsa," *Voprosy Ekonomiki*, 1950, No. 1, pp. 108–114.

Vygodskii, S. "Osnovnoi ekonomicheskii zakon sovremennogo kapitalizma," *Kommunist*, 1952, No. 22, pp. 35–52.

Yarovoi, N. "Keinsianskie retsepty dlya poslevoennoi ekonomicheskoi politiki Anglii," *Mirovaya Ekonomika i Mezhdunarodnye Otnosheniya*, 1959, No. 4, pp. 152–155.

Sources in the English language

Books, monographs, and pamphlets

Allen, J., and D. Wilkerson, eds. *The Economic Crisis and the Cold War*. New York, 1949.

Andrianov, S. N., and L. N. Sorokina. *Textbook of Economic Translation*. Moscow, 1961.

Balakian, Anna. *Surrealism*. New York, 1959.

Beveridge, W. H. *Full Employment in a Free Society*. New York, 1945.

Eaton, John. *Marx Against Keynes*. London, 1951.

Foster, William Z. *The Twilight of Capitalism*. New York, 1949.

Guillebaud, Claude W. *The Economic Recovery of Germany*. London, 1939.

Harris, Seymour E., ed. *The New Economics*. New York, 1950.

Harrod, Roy F. *The Life of John Maynard Keynes*. New York, 1951.

Keynes, John Maynard. *The Economic Consequences of the Peace*. New York, 1920.

―――. *The General Theory of Employment, Interest and Money*. London, 1936.

―――. *How to Pay for the War*. London, 1940.

Mantoux, Etienne. *The Carthaginian Peace*. London and New York, 1946.

Marx, Karl. *Capital, A Critique of Political Economy*. 3 vols. Moscow, 1954–1962.

Stalin, J. V. *Works*. 13 vols. Moscow, 1952–1955.

Varga, E. S. *The Decline of Capitalism*. London, 1928.

Varga, E. S., and Leon Trotsky. *The International Situation and Our Problems*. Moscow, 1921.

Veritas Foundation. *Keynes at Harvard*. New York, 1960.

Journals and newspapers

Amlie, Thomas R. "Full Employment After the War," *The Nation*, Supplement, CLVII (November 27, 1943), 625–652.

Johnson, Alvin. "The Economist in a World in Transition," *American Economic Review*, XXVII (March, 1937), 1–3.

Keynes, John Maynard. "The Policy of Government Storage of Food-stuffs and Raw Materials," *The Economic Journal*, XLVIII (September, 1938), 449–460.

————. "Relative Movements of Real Wages and Output," *The Economic Journal*, XLIX (March, 1939), 34–51.

————. "Trotsky on England," *The Nation and the Athenaeum*, XXXVIII (March 27, 1926), 884–885.

————. "The United States and the Keynes Plan," *The New Republic*, CIII (July 29, 1940), 156–159.

Lyubimov, N. N., and A. N. Erlikh. "The 1922 Genoa Conference," *International Affairs*, 1963, No. 6, pp. 65–70.

Makower, H., and H. W. Robinson. "Labour Potential in War-Time," *The Economic Journal*, XLIX (December, 1939), 626–640.

The New York Times, July 30, 1961.

Index